MANAGEMENT BASICS

A TO Z

MANAGEMENT BASICS

A TO Z

HOW TO ACHIEVE SUCCESS IN YOUR FIRST MANAGEMENT POSITION

DOUGLAS J. WEST

iUniverse, Inc.
Bloomington

Management Basics A to Z
How to Achieve Success in Your First Management Position

iUniverse books may be ordered through booksellers or by contacting:

iUniverse
1663 Liberty Drive
Bloomington, IN 47403
www.iuniverse.com
1-800-Authors (1-800-288-4677)

Because of the dynamic nature of the Internet, any web addresses or links contained in this book may have changed since publication and may no longer be valid. The views expressed in this work are solely those of the author and do not necessarily reflect the views of the publisher, and the publisher hereby disclaims any responsibility for them.

Any people depicted in stock imagery provided by Thinkstock are models, and such images are being used for illustrative purposes only.

Certain stock imagery © Thinkstock.

ISBN: 978-1-4759-5506-4 (sc)
ISBN: 978-1-4759-5508-8 (e)
ISBN: 978-1-4759-5507-1 (dj)

Library of Congress Control Number: 2012919103

Printed in the United States of America

iUniverse rev. date: 10/30/2012

For my loving family—my wife, Norma Jean; my sons, Corey, Steven, and Jason; and my grandson, Justin

Contents

About the Author

Doug West spent the first twenty-five years of his career in various positions at the Albany-based Pepsi-Cola Bottling Company, a franchisee of PepsiCo, Inc., maker of Pepsi-Cola and many other popular beverages. He worked his way up the corporate ladder as the company grew from roughly sixty employees working out of one facility to a business with more than six hundred employees in fifteen Pepsi franchise markets. West held senior operations and sales management positions vital to the growth of the company.

Other key positions included the management of high-profile markets for Canteen Vending, a division of Compass Group PLC, which provided food and vending services for the White House, the Smithsonian, Georgetown University, and other prestigious clients in Washington, DC.

In 2002, West obtained his real estate license and went on to get his broker's license. He currently works at the Leary Management Group, a property management company, and has served in a variety of senior managerial positions.

West's career responsibilities over the past forty years have often focused on turning poorly managed and unprofitable companies into efficient, profitable businesses, affording him the opportunity to hire, train, coach, and manage hundreds of managers and staff personnel. The knowledge he has gleaned over these past four decades in business serves as the basis of this book's discussions of basic management principles, concepts, and philosophies designed to help individuals achieve success as managers.

Acknowledgments

No book can be written alone. It takes teamwork and support for an author to usher a concept from the idea stage to the final product. First and foremost, I want to thank my wife, Norma Jean, for her steadfast patience during the nearly four years I spent bringing this project to fruition.

I owe a debt of gratitude to Bill and Steve Leary, principals of the Leary Management Group, for giving me the opportunity to field-test the key management concepts highlighted in these pages within the context of real-life situations in a vibrant corporate setting with employees who were anxious to learn the basics of management as their careers progressed within the company. The feedback I received from everyone proved invaluable during the editorial process.

Thanks to Bill and Steve and to the following members of the Leary Management Group for all of your assistance: Jaclyn Corigliano, Joseph M. Dalton, Melanie Figueroa, Meg Fitzgerald, Jeff McKinley, Sherry McMahon, and Kim Unger.

Thanks also to the editorial staff at iUniverse. You all were extremely helpful.

Introduction

Building a successful career as a manager is a bit like building a house. You need a solid foundation, quality construction materials, and a whole team of laborers and specialists to bring everything together to create the home you want. But before the first backhoe arrives at the home site, another key element must already be in place—the blueprint. That all-important document provides the information that is necessary to see the project through from start to finish. If you don't have a blueprint, you can't proceed with the job at hand.

The same thing goes for careers, especially in management. You need to start with a blueprint that you can use to lay a solid foundation for success as you enter into your first management position, and you must have a working knowledge of the basic managerial job functions. Hiring, managing, and firing employees immediately come to mind when you think of management in any form. Providing leadership to part of a company (or an entire business), whether it's the sales department or an aspect of product development, is also an obvious management function, as is keeping track of budgets and profits. Not so obvious is the need to understand human nature, identify avenues of improvement within an established business, and see how to best fit all the various pieces of the management puzzle together in such a way that you're maximizing profits without sacrificing the quality of your products and services. That's all part of management, even when you're just starting out.

As a new manager, or as a person who is seeking to enter a management career, you'll need to master a number of job functions and skills that may not be familiar to you—hiring, training, motivating, firing, logistics, scheduling, quality control, budgeting, inventory management, troubleshooting, customer service, and more all fit under the management umbrella. In fact, I can almost guarantee that you've got much to learn. I've managed multimillion-dollar franchises, a beer and wine wholesale business, a soft drink distribution company, and much more throughout my career. At the height of my entrepreneurial endeavors, the companies I helped to manage employed more than six hundred people in major markets in the United States. But I didn't snap my fingers and become a skilled and successful manager overnight. I had to work at it, and you will have to work at it too. Almost none of the managers working with me over the years instinctively knew what to do and what not to do when they started out. They needed training. They needed a blueprint to follow as they went about fulfilling their job responsibilities.

Likewise, not every middle or senior manager serving in the companies I've managed was able to impart the necessary knowledge to subordinates who were climbing the proverbial corporate ladder to ensure a smooth and efficient transition from staff to management. When you promote someone, you can't wave a magic wand and turn him or her into a top-flight manager overnight. It takes a refined management-training program, a talented employee, and lots of hard work to do that. I realized this long ago, and I began developing management-training documents specific to various aspects of management basics to use in my training programs. With enough real-world beta testing and subsequent tweaking of the content, I arrived at the basic management concepts, principles, and philosophies you will find in this book.

As a new manager, you can look to *Management Basics A to Z* to help see you through your transition to a career in management. This book also contains ample information to assist you as your career advances and you take on additional responsibilities. You may have found *Management Basics A to Z* on your own, or it may have been given to you as part of the training materials you received upon your arrival in a new management position. Regardless of how you obtained this book, you should understand that the following pages will provide you with an all-important blueprint to success. I like to call that blueprint your business management design, but I'll explain that in more detail later. Apart from giving you a good grasp of the core principles that go into working as a manager, this book will help you create a business management design of your own that you can follow as you build a successful career in management. The plan will be unique to you and your specific position, and it will evolve over time as you earn promotions. This book will also help you focus on areas where mistakes often occur, especially with new managers. Knowing where the traps are will help you avoid them. That alone will go a long way in shaping your success in the future, impressing your bosses with the confidence and skill you demonstrate in your new position.

Many new managers go wrong by not taking active steps to create business management designs. They jump in with both feet and sometimes find they can't keep their heads above water. Believe me, this is more common than you think. As I've said, you need a platform to manage and lead from. You need to be prepared with a plan to guide you proactively through the anticipated and unexpected challenges you will surely encounter throughout your career. Consider all the work and research that goes into designing a car. Auto manufacturers spend fortunes in research and development on new models, and those companies that don't eventually come up with a superior design usually fail in the marketplace. Managers operating with a poor business management design, or no plan at all, are not likely to perform as well as their counterparts who operate with a solid base of knowledge in management job functions and techniques, and with a sound plan to guide them.

If you are an aspiring manager, then you're on your way to learning what you need to know to break into an upwardly mobile career path. *Management Basics A to Z* will be your guide. If you've just been promoted into management or you've just been hired as a manager for the first time, this book will give you the start you need to avoid mistakes and build a successful career in management. Feel confident in your ability to manage, and recognize that someone in your world believes in you and your abilities; you would not have been given the opportunity otherwise. Behind all successful managers was someone who once took a chance on them and their abilities to lead and manage. These seasoned managers also went through the experience of having to work their first days as new managers at some point in their careers. They made it up the corporate ladder, and you can too!

1

What Good Managers Do

Management is a very broad term, but basically it is the process of achieving company objectives through the cooperative efforts of your team. In other words, you've got to be good at getting people to do their jobs, which isn't always easy. But management means much more than that. You are managing a part of a business or an entire business; that's going to entail more than an ability to work with and motivate your subordinates.

Let's take a quick look at what a restaurant manager does. You'll see that he or she has to deal with much more than making sure good food is served to customers. As a restaurant manager, you've got to make certain the inventory of food is kept in balance with customer demand so you don't run out of a favorite item on the menu or get stuck with food that spoils because nobody ordered it. You've got to have enough cooks in the kitchen to prepare the food, and enough waitstaff to serve it. You've got to achieve a balance between scheduling your waitstaff and the ebb and flow of customer demand. You have to ensure that the facility is clean and not in violation of state codes. Customer service is paramount, so you need to have an effective training program for new hires as well as periodic meetings to keep your current staff up to date on any new policies or marketing initiatives. You have to put policies in place that spell out what employees should do when the inevitable complaint arises. In addition, you need to focus on promoting the business, and, of course, you have to track sales, expenses, and profits.

Clearly, managing a restaurant requires a variety of skill sets. It's not all about serving good food. It's about coordinating people and products. It's about advertising and marketing. It's about inventory control, customer service, and finance. In short, it's about operating a business in an efficient manner that generates profits. As a new manager, you are going to be asked to learn a new suite of skills to go along with the ones that got you the job in the first place, and you're going to face new challenges as you go about your efforts to achieve the objectives that your bosses set for you and your subordinates.

Recognize that upper management hires people because they need help in achieving their corporate goals and objectives. Managers are typically hired to manage and grow the business, as well as to hire, direct, train, coach, support, and maximize the effectiveness of non-management personnel. So it is imperative that, as a new manager, you make it your business to fully understand what goals and objectives you are expected to meet. You need to identify what's important to your bosses in terms of priorities, standards, expectations, management style, company culture, and preferred means of communication. This is what you have signed up for, and you're going to have to make it happen quickly, efficiently, and with confidence.

Know your company's mission, and understand your objectives.

The first part of your new job is to discover the objectives your bosses have in mind for you. It may sound like overly obvious advice—figure out what your boss wants and then go do it. However, you'd be surprised at how many new managers think they know what their bosses want, but haven't really taken the time to find out for sure. Once you do find out—by asking questions and confirming the answers you receive—you're in good shape to continue on to the next step: aligning your goals, priorities, standards, and attention to detail to those of your superiors. You may have more than one boss. In fact, you probably will have quite a few. Bear in mind that each may have unique priorities that you should be aware of. Remember, you were hired to make your manager's job easier and to achieve the objectives he or she laid out for you. What's important to your boss is what should be extremely important to you. It's really that simple. Just don't forget the bosses who are above your boss in the corporate food chain.

Once you've learned, absorbed, and internalized what is important to your boss and to the company's culture, and you have in mind the specific goals and objectives your boss would like you to achieve, you're on your way to success. Incidentally, I am referring to long-term visionary objectives, day-to-day operational goals, and the simple tasks your boss may ask you to do on any given day. It's a mix, just like everything else in business.

Working with your boss should be a positive experience, but it isn't always.

Your superior's direct requests should always take priority over your routine daily tasks. You never want to tell your boss you're too busy for any project—including a lunch invitation. However, if your boss reaches out to you while you're in the middle of an important project, and you believe he or she would prefer you work through your current task rather than take on the new assignment, then make sure to ask for his or her blessing. Don't just assume you know what your boss wants. Always check. In the above scenario, it's also a good idea to offer some options and alternative solutions to address the boss's new request. Remember, you were hired to make your manager's job easier and to achieve the goals and objectives that are important to him or her. The purpose of your whole professional existence is to support this person in any way that you can, even if the timing of his or her requests poses an inconvenience. Again, all of this may sound pretty obvious, but you'd be surprised how often what should be obvious gets ignored or forgotten.

Bear in mind that most directives and requests from your boss will probably be very reasonable and realistic even if they may sometimes seem irrational and impossible to accomplish. They may in fact be projects similar to what other team members have achieved in the past. You also might not be privy to all the reasons why you have been asked to perform a particular job. Some requests could even be tests to see if you're ready for a promotion.

My advice is to not have a negative knee-jerk reaction. Things are not always as they appear. Know also that some projects will be challenging and difficult to accomplish, especially if you are new on the job or new to the management team, or if you wound up in a position beyond your current abilities. Whatever the case, don't be one of those employees who publicly complains about how unfair and unreasonable his manager is. Instead, take the time to learn from your manager. Have the wisdom and maturity to seek advice and guidance from your peers and other managers who are enjoying much success with their own careers. Keep calm, cool, and collected; and if you really do need help, by all means, ask for it. Nobody expects you to know everything.

While I hate to rain on your parade a little here, I would be remiss in my duty if I did not say right up front that there will be cases in which you won't like your boss. It's not the end of the world. Many people don't like their bosses. It's also worth noting that many of your own employees won't like you simply because you have power over their lives at work. Or they may not appreciate your management style. No matter what you do, they'll quietly (or not so quietly) resent you. As a manager, you were not hired to win a popularity contest. You were hired to do a job to the best of your ability and to motivate your team to do the best that it can. Well, your boss is in the same boat. He or she may know how you feel, but as long as you do what is expected of you, your personal feelings won't matter. If you can accept that, then you'll be able to work with someone you don't like. Besides, in most cases, you'll only have to work with this person for a few years before one of you moves on.

That said, there's an exception to everything. Not every company is reputable, and not every manager is ethical—or even sane! Seriously, you may have the misfortune of running across a superior with emotional or psychological problems. He or she might have anger issues or hate the job; taking this pent-up misery out on you is nothing personal, just highly unpleasant. Communicating with anyone who fits the above descriptions is going to be tough, if not impossible. You may have to make a break for it. Below are a few things to keep in mind before you make your exit.

- There are no guarantees that a new boss at a new company will be any better than your current supervisor, or that her management style will be better suited to your personality. As you know, the grass is not always greener on the other side of the fence. In fact, once you get over that fence, you may very well find out there are nasty snakes hiding in the weeds.

- With regard to your current employer, recognize that new professional opportunities will generally present themselves when you least expect them. In other words, you might get promoted out of your current position sooner rather than later, freeing you from working with a boss you don't like or respect.

- What stage of your career life cycle are you in? Are you young and in an entry-level management position? Were you lucky to have been given your current job opportunity? If so, you may want to think twice before leaving.

- Finding a new job is always easier when you are employed. If your situation is intolerable, don't wait to be fired; get a new job before leaving. Although it may seem odd in these days of high unemployment, many companies shy away from the unemployed.

Listen, communicate clearly, and motivate your peers and subordinates.

To achieve success, you also need to learn what's important to your peers, subordinates, and customers. Understand what their hot buttons are and the best way to manage a desired outcome when interacting with them. A key early task (and an ongoing one as well) is to learn what's important to everyone you deal with, including each person on your team. Create a culture within your organization in which the entire team understands the value of learning what's important to customers and everyone else they interact with in a group effort to cohere to the company's mission and to meet the expectations and objectives you establish for them. This knowledge will help your employees to be more efficient and effective with every task they undertake. The discovery process is pretty simple. First, you have to recognize the need to do it, and you have to start asking intelligent questions. Communication is an essential aspect of your job. You need to talk with your team, your superiors, your vendors, and your customers. And then you need to listen and respond to what you are told.

Listening is especially important when someone expresses concerns or issues. Remember, if anyone takes the time to communicate a concern to you, the issue must be important to him or her. Respect and appreciate the fact that people have come to you to express grievances or to share ideas they believe have value to the company. Offer them the professional courtesy of closely listening to these messages, and thank them and empathize with them, if appropriate. They may not necessarily like or agree with the ultimate outcomes of raising their inquiries, concerns, or suggestions, but if handled correctly most people will respect your decisions and continue to respect and come to you with their ideas and concerns.

A successful manager expertly communicates his vision, the company's mission, and specific job responsibilities to employees. For example, a vital function of communicating with your team is establishing the expected minimum standards in any given position and then providing employees with the reasonable tools and resources required to ensure they are able to perform their jobs at maximum efficiency. We'll get into these very important topics in more detail later.

The most basic element of being a successful manager is getting people to do a good job for you. It's all about eliciting cooperation and teamwork to ensure that the company makes a profit. Without communication and listening to others, you can't know what is expected of you and your team, and your team can't know what you expect it to do. Imagine trying to put together a thousand-piece jigsaw puzzle if you were only given a few hundred pieces at a time to work with, and you had no picture on the box (vision) to show you what it was you were trying to build. It would be pretty tough to put the puzzle together. In fact, the task would be impossible without having all the pieces at one time.

Unfortunately, many people toil in environments where they are working without a vision or clearly defined goals and expectations. They don't possess all of the pieces (information), tools, and resources required to perform their jobs efficiently and at the minimum standards expected by their managers. That's why it's so important to stay connected with your bosses and your team at all times, especially when you first come on board. As you begin working together, go out of your way to know what is expected of you, and to provide your subordinates with the necessary information and tools to ensure their success. After all, your success depends on theirs; and some of your boss's success depends on yours.

Taking active steps to ensure your success as a new manager is the mark of a leader. If your boss gave you this book as part of your training materials, that's an excellent sign that your company takes its new managers very seriously and wants them to succeed. That should give you enormous confidence as you go forward with the learning process. If you found this book on your own, you've taken a proactive step to further yourself in the world of management. Such decisive action is what will set you apart from your more passive counterparts within the company and at competing businesses.

Do you have what it takes to be a good manager?

Good managers are excellent communicators. They have superior people skills, follow-through, and resourcefulness. They can juggle multiple tasks and acquire multiple skill sets as needed, and they are good at planning, organizing, and problem solving. The following attributes and traits are also essential:

Humility: The last thing anyone wants in a manager is a modern version of Captain Bligh. A little humility goes a long way in the leadership business.

Sense of humor: Managers who inject a little humor into their workdays and have some fun generally get much better results than managers who walk around scowling all the time. Employees are more productive and upbeat when they are relaxed and know that they can have some fun on the job.

High energy: These overachievers tend to take care of their health, and they are more physically active as a result. That translates into enhanced performance in their jobs. They can easily energize teams simply by engaging them in a conversation. They volunteer for and enthusiastically take on extra projects.

Self-motivation: These winners are always looking for business-improving ideas without having to be asked. They are not afraid to work the extra hours required to get a job done.

Dependability: A dependable manager is a real asset. You can show that you are dependable by not having to be asked more than once to do something. Take pride in getting the job done right—the first time—even when unexpected challenges come up.

Self-discipline: Self-discipline is an essential part of being a good manager. Sometimes, it's human nature to want to procrastinate, but as a manager you can't afford to. Set a good example for your employees. Be proactive and always follow through on what you say you're going to do.

Punctuality: Your superiors and subordinates will notice if you keep your schedule. If you arrive late for meetings, they'll notice that too. Punctuality counts.

Stellar customer service: Nothing is more important than the customer. Period. As a successful manager, you'll want to always put the customer's needs at the top of your priority list and deal with any complaints in an efficient and fair manner.

The attitude of a team player: Without a great team, no manager can succeed. Do what it takes to help all of your employees succeed while addressing their desires and grievances.

While some of the advice in this chapter might sound obvious (like finding out what objectives you are expected to achieve right from the start), I've found through years of management experience that even the obvious is frequently overlooked. I cannot overemphasize the importance of taking active steps to discover the true nature of your bosses' expectations. Likewise, communicating with your team to ensure that each individual knows his or her function in terms of achieving the common goal is vital to the overall success you can expect from the effort. Subordinates need to know what is expected of them, just like you need to know what's expected of you. The process requires asking questions, listening, and communicating. It requires establishing standards and policies. Managing takes teamwork!

Your number-one job, aside from serving customers to the best of your ability, is to understand what's important to your boss and what the company's mission is. You must align your objectives, goals, priorities, and standards with those of your superiors, and you must strive to make their jobs easier. Recognize the value of learning what's important to all of the people you interact with. Knowing what's important to others will help you achieve your desired results—whether you're trying to sell a product, promote an idea, or influence your boss's decision with regard to a specific policy or procedure.

As a new manager, you're embarking on an exciting path! You'll have the chance to help grow your company's business, interact with interesting people, and make a difference for your customers. At the same time, you'll begin to reap the personal and financial rewards of a new career as a manager on the way up.

Tips in a Nutshell

- Know your company's mission, and know what your boss expects of you.
- Identify the boss's priorities, standards, expectations, management style, and preferred means of communication.
- Learn what's important to everyone you deal with, especially your team and your customers.
- Listening carefully, communicating clearly, and taking decisive action when necessary are the hallmarks of a successful manager.
- Successful managers have a plan, a platform from which to lead and manage from. Be sure to develop your business management design.

2

Communication Is King

In your personal life, I'm certain that you value communication with loved ones, friends, and acquaintances, or at least I hope you do. If something bothers you, you talk it through. You encourage, coach, cheer, counsel, and advise as needed. Relationships usually fail if communication drops off the radar. Misunderstandings, hurt feelings, confusion, frustration, anger, indifference, and all kinds of other negative results occur. The same thing holds true in business. After all, you are dealing with all sorts of people, and each one is a unique individual deserving of respect and sensitivity.

At its most basic level, communication in business involves conveying information from one party to another. Meetings, phone calls, voice mail, e-mail, snail mail, video conferences, texts, reports, job descriptions, memos, minimum performance standards (MPS) documents, posters, signs, brochures, and fact sheets are all tools we use to get across the information needed to run, manage, and grow a business. But we communicate in other ways too. Facial expression, eye contact, body language, tone of voice, and choice of words all communicate how we're feeling about what we're talking about or what we're hearing from someone else. As a manager, you're a people person, and if you are not, then you need to try to be more of one as you carry out your duties. Engaging people skills in how you communicate with others can mean the difference between success and failure in your new management job.

Whenever you need to convey a message, take a little extra time to make sure you say what you really mean to say. Your message must be clear and must leave no room for misinterpretation or confusion. Encourage your team to do the same when they pass information back and forth during the course of a business day. Everyone should strive to get the message right the first time, and everyone should follow up to ensure that the message was received and understood whenever appropriate. Clear communication among all your team members will head off serious operational problems and will enhance the quality of the customer service in your unit or department. Without a doubt, almost every problem I confront on a given day can usually be traced back to a communication crime committed by someone on our team. That is why I'm so passionate about proper communications and getting a message right the first time. Don't be afraid to over-communicate. Leave nothing to the imagination.

You can shoot yourself in the foot if you and your team don't communicate clearly.

It has become obvious to me, after four decades or so in business, that most people are poor communicators and not good conduits of information. As a new manager, you must recognize that and respond accordingly, in terms of both how you manage and how you process information from subordinates, peers, and upper management.

Typically, problems arise when people do not actually say what they mean or mean what they say. It amazes me how often I encounter this in my own company. Someone who is in a hurry or who is unclear about an issue, for example, fires off a written or spoken message that leaves too much to the imagination. The essence of the message never gets from point A to point B or to point C. That sets off an unpleasant chain reaction of confusion, lost productivity, and occasionally a conflict between individuals.

Then there are the perpetual poor listeners. They sit there supposedly taking in what is said, but you can plainly see that their eyes have glazed over and they're probably thinking about almost anything but the subject matter at hand. Failing to listen carefully is as bad as failing to communicate clearly. You can't have one without the other.

This double failure is particularly dangerous when you or your team members are engaged in spirited discussions involving differences of opinion. The individuals involved may have formed strong opinions about the subject matter at hand and may thus have become stubborn and not open to new, different, and better ideas. Or they just may not be interested in learning the facts—not a very positive attitude, to say the least. As a consequence, they don't pay attention to what is being communicated; they simply wait for their time to speak. Such behavior closes the mind to the information conveyed in what could otherwise have been productive discussions that led to new business opportunities, and it should raise a red flag with you. Do you want people like that on your team?

Companies generally suffer operationally when there is a culture of limited communication among team members. This is especially problematic in larger companies in which employees work in different departments and are required to interact with and support each other professionally without the benefit of routine meetings. The lack of communication denies employees the opportunity to regularly meet and engage each others in a group setting to actively discuss and explore ideas that might help identify sales, customer service, operational opportunities, and cost-saving initiatives.

I am an advocate of staff meetings because they represent a key venue for open communication among management and staff. Of course, while I believe in over communicating, as opposed to clamming up, I don't go overboard. We all hate meetings that waste time and put us to sleep. Yet, I firmly believe that not promoting these types of meetings (held at reasonable intervals) and not acknowledging and acting on all ideas when they are brought forward ends up hurting the company right down to its core. Whenever you suppress an employee's enthusiasm for proposing new business-enhancement ideas, you handicap your ability to manage your business. Chances are, the employee will never mention another idea again, and you don't want that.

Properly run staff meetings can enhance team cohesion and communication.

It is in your best interests to promote communication in your unit or department. If you don't, you're asking for trouble. Slipping sales quotas or other performance measurements, atrocious customer service, sagging morale, infighting among employees, pervasive negativity, and staff turnover are all likely results of a lack of communication. If you allow that to happen, your superiors will correctly begin to think you don't have what it takes to succeed in management. On the other hand, a steady and clear flow of information will foster a tight team that gets the results you were hired to achieve.

The staff meeting might sound boring or unnecessary, but I am here to tell you that you risk peril if you let that key responsibility lapse. Schedule meetings with your direct reports at least every four or five weeks. You may want to schedule them more frequently if you are new to your position and have many projects on your plate, or if perhaps you are taking on a major new assignment with your staff.

Your first step should be designating someone to be the meeting secretary. That person is responsible for keeping the minutes. The minutes set down in writing the status of current projects, any salient issues or problems, and the action items that require attention or resolution prior to the next meeting. Minutes add a level of formality to the meeting that employees will respect. Informal sit-downs are more appropriate for meetings with individual employees. I keep both hard and digital copies of my minutes for future reference and to review and follow up on at my subsequent staff meetings. The addressees in my minutes are to all the people in attendance. I always list the attendees in alphabetical order to avoid giving the appearance that I favor any one individual over another, and I note the date of the meeting along with the date the minutes were sent out.

Projects are assigned to team members with expected completion dates noted. The date and time for the next scheduled meeting is also noted in the minutes. I will often list other important subject matter discussed during a meeting as "other items discussed." Finally, I copy all attendees and those who may have an interest in something discussed at the meeting but did not attend. By taking these steps, I am able to look back a year or more later and know who was at what meeting, who was assigned a particular project, who was involved in a specific policy or procedural discussion, and who was not at a meeting but received a copy of the minutes. This is useful information should you have performance issues with an employee or if you have some other concerns with a team member at a future time. You will find a sample of meeting minutes in Appendix A.

Making deadlines and being on time for meetings are the hallmarks of professionalism that will get you noticed.

Always start your meetings on time (this is a must). Make it abundantly clear to all members of your team that showing up late for meetings is unacceptable. Lateness signals disrespect for those who made the effort to prepare and arrive on time—and it wastes their time as well. Include on your minimum performance standards document a line or two about the expectation that employees will arrive on time and prepared for all meetings. When you hire someone and go over the job description, emphasize this requirement.

Start your meetings with a review of the minutes from your last gathering. This process will help team members to focus on assigned projects while updating all the attendees about the relevant projects other members are working on. Then you can discuss the new items on your agenda. Focus on the items that are most appropriate for a staff meeting. Matters that generally involve three or more team members are most efficiently discussed at staff meetings. Matters involving one or two individuals should be discussed with them directly and in private.

Maintain control over your meetings. Do not allow private conversations to persist, and keep the meetings interesting (as much as you can make business gatherings exciting). Avoid getting into lengthy discussions with one employee while the rest of your staff sits idle. Doing so demonstrates a lack of respect for other team members and wastes their time. Your team has better things to do; members don't want to listen to a lengthy private meeting between you and another individual.

After you have discussed all items on your agenda, go around the table and ask each staff member by name if he or she has any questions, concerns, or business improvement ideas he or she would like to discuss. Do not simply go through the motions of quickly asking the questions. If you do, your subordinates may think you don't really care, and they'll stay quiet when they might otherwise have contributed something valuable. Instead, actively solicit, encourage, and promote input from your team in a way that conveys that you really want to hear from them; because you do. No one is closer to your business than your subordinates. You may be surprised at the amount of useful information you'll receive from them.

Set expectations when concluding a discussion with an individual or in a group setting. This is especially vital in staff meetings. Action items need to be noted and recorded in the minutes. Determine who is going to follow up with whom, as well as when and how that follow-up will occur. Failing to set such dates for projects and tasks will usually result in jobs not being completed in a timely manner, if at all. Failure to complete these tasks will typically lead to operational issues, which then cause other tasks not to be completed as agreed, and the cycle continues. Work to create a culture where setting project commitment dates and completing tasks on time occurs naturally, like the beat of a healthy heart. Setting commitment dates is nothing more than identifying the goals and objectives that you have agreed will be achieved by a specific date.

Follow up by sending written minutes in a timely manner. I suggest doing so within forty-eight hours of each meeting because you want to lead by example, promoting a business culture that expects prompt follow-up of the work at hand.

All projects should receive priority status, even if you think they don't matter much in the big picture.

If you let on that you think a task is unimportant to complete in a timely manner, then it pretty much guarantees your employees will respond accordingly. Some projects will get delayed in favor of other work. Above all else, you want to prevent an environment in which team members arbitrarily place projects on the back burner because they deem them unimportant. All assigned projects should be treated with equal priority; after all, people somewhere in the organization will be waiting for their completion.

Set an expectation that minor routine projects will be completed within seventy-two hours or less, or by a mutually agreed-upon date. If someone believes he is unable to complete a simple project within three days, he should reach out to those expecting its completion within this time frame to discuss options and perhaps a new completion date. Wherever practical, set specific completion or commitment dates for all projects that are expected to take more than three days. Commitment dates should be reasonable for each project and agreed to by those responsible for meeting the deadlines. As noted, projects will typically not get completed in a timely manner unless commitment dates have been assigned and unless the expectation to meet those dates has been established as a performance standard in your business unit.

You and your team should know how to respond if you expect to miss a deadline.

In the rare event it becomes clear that, with the resources at hand, you'll be unable to complete a project by the commitment date, you must notify everyone who will be impacted. Obviously, you should say so well in advance of the due date, if possible. You also want to provide ideas regarding possible alternative solutions that may help facilitate the completion of the project in accordance with the original timeline. If you do that, the people associated with the project may be less likely to bust your chops. They might even cut you some slack. You will have demonstrated respect and sensitivity for the people you work with.

Your value to your manager and company is only as good as your word. If you continually fail to carry out the commitments you make to your customers, subordinates, peers, and managers, your "word value" will progressively go down. Think of this value like that of a company's stock on the stock market. Your personal "stock" value will rise and fall proportionately with your ability to deliver what you promise. Don't expect to stick around too long if you consistently drop the ball on deadlines.

Obviously, you need to make it clear to your subordinates that deadlines must be met under all but the most serious circumstances. Staff should be told to give adequate notice and offer solutions when they discover they can't make deadlines. Meeting deadlines is part of the job. Get used to them. You'll have plenty in management.

Tips in a Nutshell

- Communicate your message clearly the first time and encourage your staff to do the same.
- Failing to listen is as bad as failing to communicate. Such double failures can cause confusion and operational difficulties that cost the company money.
- Staff meetings are essential venues for communication, and they should be held once a month.
- Appoint someone to take the minutes during staff meetings. Circulate the minutes within forty-eight hours. Copy anyone who wasn't there but has an interest in the subject matters discussed.
- Include prompt and prepared attendance of staff meetings on minimum performance standards documents.
- Run staff meetings professionally. Don't allow too much small talk or have long discussions with one individual. Such discussions are best held outside of staff meetings.
- Communicate the importance of meeting commitment dates and specify what your staff should do when they expect to miss deadlines. Nothing helps a company stay focused and operate more efficiently than a culture of adherence to these very important expectations.

3

Your Management Plan

Management is both an art and a science. It is a blend of many skill sets, a solid work ethic, an ability to motivate other people, and a capacity to adapt to rapidly changing circumstances within an organization as it responds to external influences such as shifts in the marketplace and new competition. As a successful new manager, you'll have taken the time to learn your company's mission and firmly establish the objectives you are charged with accomplishing through your individual efforts and through the efforts of your team.

The next vital step as you set out in your new position is formulating a sound plan that will define what you do to accomplish the company's goals. I strongly believe that it's impossible to manage anything—whether its new-product development, warehouse operations, or providing any type of service—without a clear plan to use as a roadmap. Your team is going to rely on you for direction. It's not enough for you to know what your boss expects you to accomplish. You also have to know how you intend to direct your team to get the job done right, on budget, and in the specified time frame for each milestone leading to the ultimate realization of the goal.

Formulate your business management design.

Years ago I coined the term "business management design" to sum up the concept of having a plan that managers could use in doing their jobs. Again, the notion of formulating a plan to use as a management platform may sound obvious, but in my experience I've found that a surprising number of new managers do not consider making a formal plan to guide them in their efforts to direct the team so that collectively everyone knows what is expected and how to meet those expectations. Instead, the newbie manager takes on the "ready, fire, aim" method, which almost always results in a failure to achieve objectives. Another way of looking at what happens without a plan is to picture a Cub Scout troop wandering around in the woods without a map or a compass. The troop won't know where it is, what it is doing, or how to find its way out of the forest.

I advise you to create a working document that clearly establishes the near- and long-term objectives that you and your immediate supervisor have agreed are a top priority. Then establish the steps you need to take to get the job done. Doing so will make it much less likely that you'll act impulsively without thinking things through. Being mindful of established policies, procedures, and standards of operation within the company will stand you in good stead with your superiors and will enable you to better articulate to your subordinates what needs to be done. As I've said, aligning your priorities, expectations, and standards with those of your superiors is essential. Your business management design should take that into account.

It's important for you to realize that most new managers mess up because there is no established standard operating procedure (SOP) in hand to carry out a function or to address a given situation. Often in these cases, if there is an SOP, it is out of date or it has been ignored for so long that everyone in your department has forgotten it existed. An SOP is important for many reasons, not the least of which is that it will spell out the course of action that is expected from you and your subordinates. It's pretty hard to hold people on your team accountable for errors or slow progress if they have no idea what they're accountable for or how they should do something. One of your first tasks as a new manager should be to ensure that there is an established SOP for vital functions in your department. If there isn't, you need to formulate one and make sure everyone on your team sticks to it.

When the stuff hits the fan—and, believe me, it will at some point—most new managers react without thinking. All they want to do is put the fire out. They hose the flames with whatever they think will work to get rid of the problem. If they had anticipated the likelihood that such a problem would come up, they could have included an SOP in their business management design to fall back on in the moment of panic. At the very least, if you face such a situation, and you will, make sure to put in place an SOP that will eliminate or reduce the odds of the bad thing happening again. In other words, be proactive instead of reactive. Superior managers have an uncanny ability to foresee potential traps and then implement procedures to head off problems before anything unpleasant occurs.

I also strongly suggest that you write a document outlining the minimum performance standards you expect from your team regarding key tasks. Obviously, you should review and discuss the document with your staff to get input on the final version. Indeed, involving members of the staff will help to firmly establish your expectations in their minds, and it will help them feel invested in the document. You might also consider having each subordinate sign a copy of the minimum performance standards document. Place a signed copy in each employee's personnel file; that way if trouble arises with a given employee's job performance in the future, it can't be said that there was no clearly defined minimum performance standard. You might even want to frame the document and hang it in the lunchroom. This document is also an important component of your business management design.

As you implement your plan, strive to create a culture where policies and standard operating procedures are followed unfailingly. If a policy or SOP is outdated, then make sure to immediately modify or eliminate it. Do not allow it to sit on the books. Doing so will set a precedent for employees to pick and choose which policies and procedures they want to follow, and those they don't. Do not allow your staff to routinely ignore other rules and procedures as well. You do not want to create a culture where policies and procedures are viewed as optional. Instead, encourage your staff to offer ideas and suggested alternatives to existing procedures and policies if they feel they are cumbersome or obsolete. Then modify or eliminate policies accordingly to meet your current business needs. It's also important for you to recognize that you cannot write policies for every contingency, and that there will be times when circumstances will dictate a need to deviate from a given policy. Train and coach your team to recognize this fact and empower them to act accordingly.

Your management style will determine whether your plan succeeds or fails.

One of the keys to your success and long-term future in business is how you actually manage. Of course, you're managing people, and they can be challenging. Don't let them get your goat and do not take things personally. But you're also managing pressure, deadlines, logistics, problems, tiny details, the big picture, office politics, budgets, sales and marketing, inventory, and so much more. That sounds like a lot, and it is. But don't get discouraged. You can do this—especially with a plan in hand. Professionals routinely deal with a myriad number of pressing issues at once, and they do it with enviable aplomb, or at least they should. We call this management style, and it's critical to your ability to effectively implement your business management design. It's also critical to your ability to lead your team to yield maximum return on your collective efforts to fulfill the company's mission.

There are many different styles of managing. Some work well and are very successful, but others are not. For example, we've probably all dealt with the aloof, unapproachable boss, or the boss who wants to be popular and therefore gets nothing done, or the boss who is so overbearing and sarcastic that everyone would dance if he or she fell under a bus. Clearly, you don't want to be like that!

Your approach to managing will depend on many factors, such as your personality, level of motivation, training, and overall experience. The company's corporate culture will factor into your style as well. If you're managing an innovative team of young people in Silicon Valley, you're going to manage in a far different way than you would if you led a team of employees at an auto manufacturing facility.

Your own personal and professional goals will play a part in how you manage too. Styles vary, but I advocate for a cool, calm, and sensitive approach. Be fair and firm—not a pushover. Listen, clearly articulate what you expect, make sure you've got procedures, policies, and standards fully documented, and address employee grievances or problems quickly and decisively. And don't be afraid to praise your team for a job well done. Everybody likes to be appreciated.

Finding the best management style may take a little time, especially since you are a new manager. Don't worry if it does. Just make sure you are aware of how you interact with others—your subordinates, superiors, vendors, and customers. Try to project an easy sense of self-confidence. And recognize that you may need to alter your management style from time to time as you climb the corporate ladder in your business, or as you move to another industry or company.

Be sure to factor into your business management design a need to enjoy yourself on the job. This includes reserving adequate time for family, along with time for you to do what you enjoy most. Leading a life with a reasonable balance between your work and your leisure time will help you stay philosophical with a positive, can-do mind-set. If you're not having fun, you're not going to be a productive manager and leader, and you won't be playing at the top of your game. You certainly won't be looking at your job as a long-term commitment, and your subordinates and superiors will catch on to that really fast.

Your management style should help create a culture where employees go out of their way to achieve the goals and objectives you have set for them. Your approach and plan should encourage employees to feel comfortable with going to you and other appropriate team members with ideas that may help enhance the company's performance, or with other issues and concerns they may have. Part of your job is to learn how to graciously turn down an employee idea (if necessary) without crushing the future enthusiasm of team members. In short, you're dealing with a multitude of issues, and you need to be prepared for that. If you're happy and comfortable in your own skin, you'll project that same sense of confidence to everyone you meet.

Paying attention to details will set the course for your plan's success.

As you formulate and implement your business management design, it's important to take into account any glaring deficiencies you identify along the way. Factor in solutions to the problems you see. There will always be opportunities to increase sales, reduce expenses, and improve operating efficiencies. Among your first steps, then, should be a taking a careful look at the company itself, its inner works, its strengths and weaknesses, and the procedures that are in place to effectively reduce or eliminate costly oversights and problems.

Let's recap some points I've already made just for emphasis, and let's look into some other details you need to pay attention to.

- Become familiar with and fully understand your company's business model and mission, and know what products and services it sells and what market it serves.

- Assess how well your business unit is performing against budget with regard to sales, expenses, and net operating profit. Assuming there is a budget in place, you'll need to understand how well the company is performing compared to budget. Is the company making money? Is there positive cash flow? What are the current sales and operating expense trends? You'll need this information as you go about creating your business management design.

- Assess how well the company is performing against industry standards, your direct competitors, and your own personal standards and expectations.

Become familiar with the sales and operating expense ratios in your department (if applicable), and the expectations for providing customer services for your industry. Learn what customer services your direct competitors excel at. Learning that will help you understand just how well your company is (or should be) performing in terms of customer care, services, and satisfaction.

- Observe and assess your company's ability to function and carry out its mission, the quality of the personnel, and whether the company functions under an effective overall business management design. Are there standard operating procedures in place to help provide superior guidance to the team? Does the SOP meet the current needs of the business? Have minimum performance standards been put in place? If not, part of your plan will be to establish SOP and MPS documentation as soon as possible.

- Remember that common sense must prevail in all phases of your job. It is impossible to write policies and procedures to address every possible work-related contingency. At times situational facts and circumstances will rise to a level that will dictate a deviation from an established policy or procedure, or perhaps even a minimum standard.

  Because common sense can be subjective, do not confuse the prudent use of this rule with employees who choose to routinely ignore policies and procedures for the wrong reasons. Those individuals may require training, coaching, and possible counseling and disciplinary action to keep them from abusing this principle. The commonsense principle is an important concept that you and your team should embrace and understand. In essence, it just means you should use your head and try not to do anything really dumb.

- Begin to manage, lead, and motivate your team to make it (and you) hugely successful in carrying out your part of fulfilling the company's mission. Enjoy the fruits of your labor and have fun along the way! That's part of why you're in management!

So, you see that a business management design is really a grand plan that includes a collection of other plans and contingencies, standard operating procedures for vital functions or situations, and a clearly defined system of accountability for your team and for yourself. This entire book is a sort of business management design. It provides you with basic information you can use in formulating your own plan, and it points out areas where you can head trouble off at the pass. Of course, there are certain components of your business management design that you will need to customize to suit your personal preferences, your specific industry, and your company's current ability to function and carry out its mission.

Tips in a Nutshell

- Create a business management design (plan).
- Establish or adhere to existing standard operating procedures for functions and situations, like customer complaints. Modify or eliminate those SOPs that have become antiquated and no longer meet your current business needs.
- Establish minimum performance standards for tasks and functions. MPS documents simply contain excerpts from your established SOPs and other expectations that are important to you. These documents typically include the top ten or so performance standards that are most often ignored by employees that when not adhered to create the most havoc within an organization.
- Encourage a culture in your team that makes every employee want to go out of his or her way to achieve objectives and to follow SOPs and exceed MPS.
- Adopt a cool, calm, and sensitive management style, but be firm and fair. Never be a pushover. Respond to employee problems, issues, or ideas quickly and with sensitivity.

- Do not be overly zealous and rigid with procedures and policies to the point that they paralyze your team's ability to carry out your company's business in an efficient and practical manner. Remember the commonsense principle, it must always prevail.

4

Hiring Employees

As I've indicated already, managers have to possess multiple skill sets to do their jobs right. The more responsibilities you have, the more this is the case. The bigger the company you work for, the more bureaucracy you'll face in your daily routine, which will require you to skillfully navigate in a way that does not alienate subordinates, peers, and superiors while still pushing your unit toward achieving its objectives. But no matter if you are working in your own business, for a small company, or for a giant corporation, the one skill you must have in order to succeed in management is an ability to understand and motivate the people on your team. People skills are also incredibly important when going through the hiring and firing process. If you have a human resources department, you'll be spared from some of the more mundane aspects of these essential personnel functions, but you'll still be involved, perhaps even more than you think at this point.

Understanding people: This is a broad subhead, and I use it deliberately because it represents the big basket of elements that go into effective leadership. The umbrella of understanding people really gets to the core of what it takes to be a superior leader.

If you don't understand people, then you can't lead them. It's as simple as that. You can try to lead them, but they'll see right through you, and then they may resist you in overt or covert ways. They'll know you don't understand or perhaps don't care about them, and they won't like it one bit. I've seen this play out time after time, and it isn't pretty. Ultimately, managers of this sort are proven ineffective and removed, or they run—mumbling to themselves on the way out.

Let me also say right here that if you can't, don't, or won't understand yourself, then you can't effectively manage others. Managers, at least the good ones, must be self-assured and secure within their own skins. The compass that drives us has to be an inner one that has come from experiencing life and accepting that it is not only sometimes unfair, but also highly unpredictable. In many ways, business mirrors life. It, too, is often unfair and unpredictable. It's helpful to realize that from the get-go. As exceptional managers, we didn't rise through the ranks because someone handed us an opportunity for no good reason. We rose because we understood and respected most everyone we came into contact with inside and outside the company and because we understood what was expected of us and how to get it done with the loyal and committed support of our team members.

We know we can't look to others to make us feel like we belong, that we're valuable as human beings, and that we have something to contribute. We have to know that we are all these things and more! Articulate, smart, firm, confident, diplomatic, sensitive, perceptive, assertive (when necessary), creative, adaptive, and resourceful are among the adjectives I would ascribe to what I would call the profile of a successful manager. Those who have these traits or who can cultivate them over time will operate from a sense of self that will translate into accurately reading other people and being able to understand why they act as they do, either for good or bad, within the company. This is extremely relevant when it comes to hiring and firing employees.

Motivating people: We have discussed the importance of motivating your team in earlier chapters. In the context of hiring and firing, motivation takes on a new wrinkle of sorts. It becomes very important at the beginning and end of a person's relationship with the company insofar as a motivated new hire is more likely to succeed than an unmotivated one, and an underperforming employee who is motivated to change is less likely to get fired than an underperforming employee who doesn't care one way or the other. As a manager, it's your job to psych your team up and to keep each member of it as excited and committed as possible. If problems arise with an underperforming employee, your ability to motivate him or her to take corrective action could end up saving you lots of money that would otherwise be spent on hiring someone else to fill the position.

As a new manager, chances are, you're going to inherit your team, but as time passes you're going to have a hand in shaping it. As a matter of course, people will quit, get promoted, transfer, and retire. New people will join the team from elsewhere in the company, or they'll be brought in from outside the company. Get involved as this natural personnel cycle plays itself out in your business unit. With every shift, you have the ability to make important adjustments to enhance productivity, performance, and profits.

Let's take a close look at the hiring process first. Then in the next chapter we'll move on to the tricky dance you'll sometimes have to do when it comes time to fire an employee—without causing costly legal trouble for yourself and the company.

Employee turnover can be very expensive and disruptive to your business. Try to get the hiring process right the first time out of the gate.

The press of business can often lead to a common mistake when a position becomes vacant and must be filled. The tendency is to hire the first warm body that comes through the door. As intelligent managers, we know that doing so is foolish, but sometimes we do it anyway. In spite of the temptation, don't replace a flat tire with a bald tire. You'll be sorry sooner rather than later. Taking shortcuts (not properly searching for and screening prospective new hires) perpetuates poor personnel performance and turnover problems, and these generally result in a continuation of other operating issues and ongoing distractions in the entire business unit.

Consider these points:

- The hard costs and extra effort associated with recruiting, hiring, and training new personnel add up fast.

- The soft costs and possible loss of revenue associated with the expected disruption of business activity will hurt you personally as your unit suffers. Your superiors will definitely notice what's going on.

- The likely decline in the quality of customer care and services will reduce the profitability of your department. Customers are like elephants. They have long memories, and they'll most likely go elsewhere if they become angry enough. It costs money to get new customers, so that expense must also be factored into the equation.

- Some competent employees will leave when they see that you are not managing the unit properly, and the inevitable brain drain that occurs will just add more stress to your day and contribute to a further decline in performance and profitability.

You want to hire people for the long term, not as temporary Band-aids. It is in your best interest to do it right the first time, and you want to hire the best employees your budget will allow. Surround yourself with very competent people—preferably, people who are much smarter than you. Take the time to find candidates who are coachable, have direct work-related experience and the technical skills you seek, and whose personalities are compatible with your team. Obviously, you also want to make sure the person does not have a history of drug abuse, theft, violence, job hopping, or absentee issues.

Hiring someone is like getting married after only one or two dates, so invest some quality time in vetting the candidate before you say, "You're hired." Or you may soon be saying, "You're fired!" As in a marriage, you want to hire someone with the intention that it will be for life. In other words, you want a great partner. You want someone who is as passionate and committed to your company's mission and goals as you are.

It should go without saying that you and your hiring team must be familiar with current federal and state labor laws. A very basic example is that you can't discriminate (not hire someone) based on race, gender, religion, or age, to name a few. An uninformed manager can get the company in hot water with a slip of the tongue if he or she isn't up on the latest laws.

If your company does not have an HR department, look for seminars and government websites that feature federal and state employment and labor laws. Every team member who is involved in the interviewing, hiring, and managing of employees should receive basic training and possess a working knowledge of what is acceptable and what is not when it comes to hiring, managing, and firing employees. When in doubt, consult a good labor attorney. Lawsuits are expensive. Avoid them.

Standardizing the hiring process makes good business sense.

To facilitate hiring the right person to fill a vacancy, develop a comprehensive, standardized process and ensure that your team adheres to it. This will also help minimize your exposure to potential lawsuits due to unlawful hiring practices. There are many different approaches to hiring new employees. Consider the following as you develop a standardized process of your own:

- Define the minimum requirements and standards for the job as well as your expectations of the new employee— minimum education, technical training, job-specific experience, and so on.

- Develop a well-written job description that fully outlines the scope of the job. (See Appendix A for a sample job description.)

- When recruiting starts, the hiring process should include two separate interviews conducted by two different managers. The hiring manager should be responsible for, or at least involved in, the process for hiring his or her direct reports. If I'm available, I prefer to be the second manager to interview a prospective new employee.

- If the initial interviews qualify the candidate as a potential new hire, verify employment references and the person's educational background prior to making an offer.

- When making the offer, inform the potential new hire that the offer is subject to a drug test, criminal background check, and verification of a valid driver's license (if necessary). I also suggest you review the person's driving record. Excessive speeding, red-light running and unpaid parking tickets can speak volumes about one's character.

- Consider running a credit check if the candidate is going to work in sensitive areas of the company.

Promoting from within offers many benefits, but it's not always the right choice.

Some managers like to bring in new blood from outside the company when a position opens up, and there's nothing wrong with that. In fact, hiring from outside has its advantages. For one thing, the new hire hasn't been influenced by the existing corporate culture, which may be in need of adjustment. The person won't be embroiled in office politics or the tribalism that can sometimes develop in poorly run enterprises. They will come to the company fresh, motivated and with new ideas to carry out their job functions. The simple fact of the matter is that there might not be any existing employees who can fulfill those job functions as well, which makes hiring from the outside a necessity.

I personally like to promote from within a company if it is at all feasible. You avoid creating dissention in the ranks, and you build team morale. Consider giving the job description for the vacant position a careful read to see if there is anyone who is currently working for the company that could be promoted. I find it's well worth the effort. It saves on recruitment costs (advertisements and headhunters), background checks, and the time-consuming process of interviewing.

The benefits of promoting from within should be considered seriously:

- Promoting from within boosts employee morale and helps to retain select talent. Ambitious and efficient employees will ultimately leave if they don't feel there is room for advancement in the company. If these employees see there is opportunity to rise in the ranks, they'll be more likely to stay and work harder. After all, an employee's first loyalty is to himself or herself. The person is working toward achieving individual professional and financial goals. Never forget that!

- Promoted employees possess valuable information specific to your business unit that enables them to take on new responsibilities proactively, thereby making meaningful contributions to your organization in a shorter period of time than new hires could.

- Promoted employees possess institutional knowledge that can enhance efficiency and productivity when applied in new job functions within the company.

While promoting from within is most desirable in my view, it may not always be in the best interest of the company. You need to determine if business conditions—not just your personal preferences—will allow for promoting a specific individual at a given time. For example, denying a promotion of my long-term administrative assistant because it might be hard and inconvenient for me to find and train a replacement as good as she is would be selfish. I would never hold somebody back for selfish reasons, and neither should you. It would be the wrong reason not to promote an employee, and it would certainly be a morale buster once word got out. And you can bet the word would get out too! The bottom line is that you should not penalize someone because he or she does an awesome job. When business conditions allow, promote personnel to also promote the best interests of your company.

However, that being said, I will hold back an individual if current business conditions won't allow promoting him or her from within at a given time. Take a customer service rep in a sensitive position. He or she has been in that position for less than a year, and there has been significant turnover in that department. Removing an employee who is just getting established in terms of procedures and knowledge would prolong the lack of stability in this department. The department would experience an orchestrated brain drain with you as the misguided conductor.

In the above scenario, I'd have to deny the promotion, which might not be all that fair to the employee but would be in the best interest of the company. The person would receive the utmost consideration in the future, though. I prefer that employees work in their current positions for at least one year before considering promotions. The employee must be in good company standing, and he or she must also be capable of expertly teaching a new hire how to do the job he or she will be leaving.

The process of hiring outside the company can be arduous and time consuming, but when you find the right employee you've hit a home run!

In these days of high unemployment, it is not uncommon for dozens or even hundreds of candidates to vie for a single job at a company. For job seekers, the situation is often demoralizing, to say the least. For you as a new manager, it is a real hassle because every Tom, Dick, and Harry is going to apply. You'll get deluged with résumés, all of which have to get sorted out. If you have an HR department, thank your lucky stars. The people in HR will take care of the arduous tasks and find you a pool of qualified candidates. If you don't have an HR pro on staff, you'll have to wear that hat as well.

Print and online ads will generate leads, perhaps too many.

While you'll have to direct the hiring effort, there's no reason why you have to do everything. Delegate some of the tasks to trusted subordinates if and where appropriate. For example, have a subordinate write the online job posting and pass it to you for approval. Sifting through the pile of résumés that will result from virtually any form of advertising is another job that can be delegated.

Here are a few tips you might want to consider as you get the process going:

- Check out your local newspaper and online sites to learn what your competitors are offering in terms of salary for a similar position and how they are crafting their ads. Write your ad accordingly. Delegate this task.

- Do not list a phone number in your ad. Ask applicants to e-mail or fax their résumés. Discard all that don't meet the minimum standards you specified in your hiring plan.

- Utilize various ad filters to manage incoming résumés. For example, list your address or preferably a landmark close to where the new hire will work. The idea here is to encourage applicants living near your company's location to submit résumés and discourage those who do not. Other filters might include listing required experience, education, hours of work, and so forth. Depending on the job opening and other circumstances, there may be times when you'll simply want to cast a wide recruiting net and list your ad with few, if any, filters. Just realize that fewer filters means more wasted time going through résumés that don't fit the job.

Please see Appendix A for a sample employment ad with filters (qualifiers) built in. At the very least, it might spark some ideas as you craft your own ad.

You'll get lots of résumés, so process them quickly to find potential interviewees.

I suggest that, as résumés come in, you review and sort them based on the following factors:

- Is the résumé neatly organized and easy to read and understand? If not, toss it. Ditto if it contains typos or grammatical errors.

- Does the applicant live near your business location? If not, I generally move on. However, I have hired people who didn't live nearby when their résumés reflected exceptional qualifications and I was having difficulty finding local talent at that given time.

- Does the applicant meet the minimum education and job-related experience requirements?

- Is the applicant a job hopper? Lack of longevity can be a bad sign.

I quickly process the first round of résumés to determine which ones get tossed based on the above criteria. I'll take a minute or two to look over the keeper résumés. I mark the top of the résumés with a yellow highlighter; the farther the yellow mark is to the right margin, the more interested I am in giving the applicant an in-depth look. Then I do a final review, select the top three, and give the applicants a call.

I do a relatively short phone interview with the applicants, but I make sure I spend enough time to get a feel for the individual's technical experience, desired wage range, and his or her personality before deciding whether I want to invite the person in for a face-to-face interview. If I am not yet sure about asking the prospect in for an interview, I'll tell the candidate that I have more phone interviews to do and that I will call back if I have continued interest in him or her. If I like the prospect at the conclusion of the call, I immediately set up an in-office interview.

When conducting an initial office interview, I ask open-ended questions to get the applicant talking. Below is a list of standard questions that I ask every applicant, which you might want to ask your applicants too. Add additional questions to a standardized interview approach of your own.

Are you currently working?
If not, what was your last job, and when did you leave?
Why did you leave before finding a new job?
What do you consider to be your strengths for this position?
What do you consider to be your weaknesses?

After asking questions about the individual's education and past employment history, I zero in on each previous job, the job responsibilities, the applicant's likes and dislikes about each job, earnings, and the reason the person left each position. I try to determine career patterns and how the applicant thinks and articulates his or her thoughts, the level of technical skills they possess that are relevant to the position, and his or her personality.

Does the applicant appear coachable, career minded, and likely to fit in with the rest of the team?

Is the person actively selling me on why I should hire him or her?

Douglas J. West

Interviews can turn up red flags you should not necessarily ignore.

The following would raise red flags during an interview:

- Inaccurate résumés indicate the applicant might be lazy, untrustworthy, or disorganized, or takes very little pride in his or her work.

- Candidates who leave a job on their own prior to lining up new employment always concern me. Most responsible people who have bills to pay and a family to support do not usually leave one job without first securing new employment elsewhere. There could have been major problems with the previous employers, or the applicants may have encountered significant issues in their personal lives. Find out what the deal was. The candidate may have had a legitimate reason to hastily leave a job, or he or she may have been asked to resign in lieu of being fired.

- If a candidate has been actively seeking employment for a relatively long period of time without success, this might suggest that the applicant lacks motivation, initiative, creativity, and the ability to get the job done. It's a hard fact of life today that employers look on the long-term unemployed with suspicion even if that's grossly unfair. You need to find out as much as you can during the interview. Perhaps there is nothing to worry about. Just be sure. For example, I usually ask how active the applicant has been in his or her search for employment. I also ask the individual to assess the current job market, what the applicant is personally experiencing, and why he or she thinks the search has yielded no results thus far. The answers to these questions can tell you a lot about the potential new employee.

- Unemployed applicants seeking positions that are much lower in pay or stature than they are accustomed to are also worrisome. Be mindful that candidates accepting jobs significantly lower in pay may accept your offer of employment with absolutely no intention of sticking around for long. They are simply in survival mode and desperate to pay the bills. Some of these applicants are savvy enough to realize that it's always easier to find new employment when a job seeker is currently employed. Consider the costs and amount of effort required to hire and train your new employee when making hiring decisions under these circumstances.

When you identify a potential new member of your team, spend some extra time during the interview describing the job and the company in detail.

In most cases, you'll know pretty quickly if you're not likely to offer the applicant the job. Do keep an open mind, though. I've seen interviews that started out rough proceed to an offer because the candidate was able to recover. At any rate, if at the end of the standardized portion of the interview, you know the person isn't right for the position, give a short description of the job and end the conversation.

If the candidate is of interest, then go into more details about what he or she would be doing in the company. I know it sounds a little devious, but I typically make the job sound a bit more challenging than it actually is. I'd rather scare someone off before they actually come to work for me. This tactic increases the odds that my new hire will be happy with the new job, and that he or she will be more likely to stay on our team for the long term. You don't want to sugarcoat a job in an effort to coax an individual into a position that he or she would not otherwise accept. Individuals hired under those circumstances will usually become unhappy employees who will soon begin to look for other work.

In closing the interview, I ask the applicant if he or she is still interested in being considered for the job and if he or she has any additional questions. I thank the applicant for coming in and indicate that I still have other interviews scheduled and that I will contact him or her once a decision has been made. If the candidate is someone

I'm highly interested in, I say so, indicating that the next steps will involve reference and other background checks, and possibly another interview.

Sometimes you have to go with your gut if you can't get much information from an applicant's references.

A few words on references are in order. In the old days, most employers were happy to discuss former employees, or at least those who had left on good terms. Now, though, many employers are aware that the slightest slip of the tongue can land the company in the middle of a lawsuit. Don't be surprised if you get stonewalled when you call references. In most cases, you'll be lucky if you can even confirm the applicant's dates of employment and job title, and verify if the candidate resigned or was laid off.

In smaller companies, you might find managers who are unaware of the potential legal pitfalls involved in answering questions about former employees. At a minimum, I ask the reference if he or she would hire the applicant again. The answer to that question is usually very telling about the potential new employee. If references are good, I call the candidate and make an offer. If I'm unable to get a reference, I make a business decision based solely on the information I have learned about the prospect. If I believe the candidate is qualified and possesses the skills, character, and other traits I'm looking for, I take a chance and make an offer. After all, we only call references in an effort to validate our own assessment of a prospective employee. That is to say, references are simply one piece of information I factor into my decision to hire someone.

Also, bear in mind that there are times when reference providers (giving good or bad reviews) may have their own agendas. They could be biased against or in favor of your applicant, so always treat their opinions accordingly.

As a new manager, you'll be amazed at what a thorough interview and background check can turn up. Many years ago I was concluding an interview, and at the end I said that, if we made an offer, the hiring would be subject to a drug test and a criminal background check. The guy thought for a minute, and then he asked, "Uh, about the drugs. Does pot count?"

After a while, nothing will surprise you about the people who come in looking for jobs. It's a crazy world out there! Sometimes you've just got to smile at the absurdity of it all.

Tips in a Nutshell

- Knowing federal and state labor laws and following your company's standard procedures for hiring personnel will help prevent costly lawsuits.
- Understanding yourself and others enables you to lead effectively.
- Just hiring a warm body will end up costing you more money than taking the time to hire the right person in the first place.
- Write job descriptions and interview questions as you develop a standardized hiring process.
- Include filters (qualifiers) in the employment ads you post.
- Don't ignore red flags in interviews, but keep an open mind.
- Conduct criminal background checks, check references (when possible), and require drug testing.

5

Firing Employees

Despite your best efforts when hiring new employees and managing existing staff members, the day will inevitably come when you will have to fire an individual on your team. It's never pleasant. You know the individual needs the job to pay the light bill and that in all probability it's not going to be easy for him or her to get another position right away. As a manager, you should be highly sensitive to the fact that getting fired is an extremely traumatic event for most people; as such, the process needs to be undertaken with compassion, caring, an adherence to all company procedures, an awareness of federal and state labor laws, and the knowledge that such action represents an absolute last resort.

Chances are, the employee brought the termination on himself or herself and knows that deep down. But there are bound to be hard feelings anyway, possibly fireworks, so be prepared for that eventuality. Just as nothing will surprise you once you get used to the hiring process, nothing will surprise you when it's time to let someone go. The person may cry. He or she may beg for just one more chance—or stare at you as if you've just whacked them over the head with a Louisville Slugger. The person may protest that the firing is unjust or simply storm out of the office. In all seriousness, you will want to have two company representatives in the room at the time of termination. These reps' presence will help ensure everyone's safety and corroborate what was or was not said should questions be raised at some point in the future.

Another key point I want to make is that prior to taking the drastic action of firing someone, a solid and prolonged period of self-examination on your part would not be remiss. Should you blame yourself because an employee just couldn't cut the proverbial mustard? Maybe. Did you give the employee all the tools he or she needed to do the job? Was the job description clear? Did the employee require additional support that wasn't provided, even though it should have been? Were you asking the employee to work over his or her skill level? Did you repeatedly inform the employee of what exactly was lacking in his or her job performance, and did you try to motivate the person to take corrective action?

It's easy to blame the employee, and it's hard to blame yourself. If you're at fault, then that means you were the one who was falling down on the job, just as much as the person you are firing. If you realize that you are at fault, that's a good thing because you'll be able to address the problem areas in your management style and procedures so that you won't find yourself in a similar situation in the future. You'll probably still have to fire the employee, though. The damage will already have been done, and that's something you'll just have to live with. Believe me, missteps happen all the time when managing personnel. As a new manager, you will make mistakes, and some of them will be painful. Just realize that you've made an error in judgment or in management technique, and/or that you hired the wrong individual, and move on. Vow to avoid making the same mistake twice.

If you identify an underperforming employee, take immediate action to solve the problem. If remediation doesn't work, then termination is your only option, but it should be a last resort.

Putting emotions and psychology aside, your first duty as a manager is to your team and your company. If a member of your team is hindering everyone else's ability to function at top efficiency, then that person is a liability to you, your team members, other employees in the firm, vendors, customers, and stockholders (if the business is a publicly traded company). Don't sit idle while underperforming employees are actively engaged in your business unit. Take the appropriate action that will result in a positive outcome for the company as a whole. As noted, the ideal outcome would be that the employee is properly coached and counseled, and his or her work performance rises to a level that is acceptable to you and your superiors.

So, once you spot an underperformer, the first step is to make an effort to correct the performance deficiencies in a positive, efficient, and timely manner. Do not simply ignore the problem or hastily fire someone because you don't believe the employee is worth saving from the ax. And don't fire because you feel you do not have the time to properly address a poorly performing employee. You might think you have more important things to do, but managing your team is one of your top responsibilities. Bear in mind that reasons such as the ones I just shared are what I hear from lazy or incompetent managers who never last long in my companies. Trust me. Your superiors will have heard similar excuses, and if you are foolish enough to offer them, your bosses are quickly going to start taking a hard look at your personnel track record. Always remember that a dysfunctional team, excessive turnover, and a lack of efficiency will ultimately rest on your shoulders.

The above ill-advised approaches—waiting too long to address employee problems, firing too hastily, and failing to try corrective action—will usually cause a variety of short- and long-term difficulties for the entire organization, including potential wrongful-discharge lawsuits, employee morale issues, and high employee turnover. On the upside, taking a proactive and sensitive approach to correctly manage subpar employees will provide numerous benefits:

- It is almost always less expensive to save an existing employee than to hire and train someone new. And if that's not enough incentive for you to address the problem with coaching and counseling, then consider that there is no guarantee that your new hire will be an improvement over the employee you just fired. In fact, the person could be even worse! That would be highly irritating, wouldn't it? So, make a sincere effort to work with what you have first—before starting over again.

- It is less disruptive to your business unit when you are able to minimize employee turnover. A stable labor force is a sign of a good manager. If you have one, preserve it. The benefits will accrue to the company and to you personally as you are recognized as a superior leader. Promotions will follow. Conversely, if you are seen as an inept leader whom nobody wants to work for, you will probably be shown the door.

- Disruptions in personnel impact the daily operations of your department or business unit, but they also taint your staff. Typically, a malcontent is going to verbally undermine you at every turn to anyone who will listen; and, sadly, plenty of your subordinates will hang out by the water cooler to dish the dirt with that malcontent. Further, when you terminate the underperformer, somebody will have to do the person's job until you fill the position. That will breed further discontentment in the ranks. Your best employees may jump ship, and your department will face a brain-drain problem that will be very difficult to reverse once it gets going.

Remember, the longer your people work for you and the company, the more institutional knowledge they bring to the party. Such knowledge and history are very valuable, and they shouldn't be thrown away lightly.

- Adhering to a constructive, fair, and deliberate process for correcting employee deficiencies will help maintain favorable employee morale. Happy and productive employees are less likely to look elsewhere for work, complain about the boss at the watercooler, call in sick a lot, and surf the Web when they should be doing their jobs. All of those positives come together to notch your team up to peak efficiency.

Negative managers get noticed just as quickly as positive managers. Fostering negativity can get you fired, whereas fostering a positive culture of caring, efficiency, and hard work in your department or business unit will get you promoted. Keep that in mind the next time a subordinate totally ticks you off and you are tempted to break out the ax!

When you finally must terminate an employee after trying everything to avoid it, you need to follow company procedures and labor laws to discourage potential lawsuits.

In all my years in management, I've come to believe in many things. When it comes time to fire an employee, I believe that my resorting to such drastic action should come as no surprise to the person. He or she isn't going to like it, of course, but the firing won't come out of the blue if you handle the entire process correctly as soon as you begin addressing the problem of an underperforming employee.

Here's what I mean in a little more detail: As you've seen, my preferred method for managing personnel challenges is to practice the art of progressive discipline and counseling, which typically includes some coaching and training. I will get into progressive discipline and counseling in more depth in the section below, but suffice it to say here that I do all I can to save employees instead of summarily firing them for poor performance. At the end of the evaluation, counseling, coaching, and training process, the employee will have come to understand my concerns. If the individual has been unwilling or unable to ramp up his or her efforts to show more competence in the job, then getting fired isn't going to be surprising. In a sense, I professionally counsel these types of employees right out the door, with no regrets on my part. The employee will also be less likely to make a scene, which is a good thing. When done correctly, the formal process should take no longer than ninety days from start to finish. But mark my words. It's never easy, which is why many managers don't bother with it and consequently suffer negative impacts on their careers.

To recap, unsatisfactory job evaluations should lead to further communication with the employee to determine why his or her performance fails to meet the minimum standards specified for the job. The employee may very well believe he or she is doing just fine, so it's your responsibility to clearly articulate why you disagree. The employee may reveal personal troubles that are affecting his or her job, and you'll have to work together to see how to address whatever issues are degrading performance. The next step is further coaching, more detailed supervision, counseling, and possibly additional training. A second bad evaluation could lead to putting the employee on notice for possible termination. The last step is termination.

If your company does not have standardized procedures for dealing with and terminating problem employees, meet with your immediate supervisor and tactfully bring up the issue. Listen carefully to what you are told and, if appropriate and authorized by your manager, begin to implement a system on your own. It need not be overly formal; but your procedures should be in writing, and you must be consistent in administrating your new policies.

Including a system for firing (and hiring, for that matter) in your business management design is a good idea. As a savvy manager, you understand that you sometimes have to act and think outside the box to properly manage your people.

Douglas J. West

Progressive discipline and counseling are important tools when dealing with underperforming employees.

What are progressive discipline and counseling? I've already alluded to both in the above paragraphs, but I'll share a more in-depth look. Both concepts are very important for you to embrace as you develop your business management design in your new position. In my view, we are looking at two different disciplines that require separate discussions.

Progressive discipline: The idea behind this concept is that you will no doubt encounter employees who may be very competent and generally good at their jobs but exhibit behavior that requires your attention. For example, some employees may have attendance issues; they might routinely ignore company policies and procedures; or they may not play well with others. They might violate company dress codes, show up late for meetings, or take excessively long breaks. They might surf the web, check their Facebook pages, or make numerous personal calls on company time. Sadly, the list is virtually endless. You'll be amazed at the excuses you'll get, the justifications for bad behavior, and the denial of the same. The "My dog ate my homework" excuse for missing a deadline may sound absurd in a corporate setting, but believe it or not, I've heard even sillier ones than that!

All of these things are going to annoy you to no end, but keep in mind that most people really would rather be anywhere else than at work—and they would be, if they had enough money to lead lives of leisure. On some days, you probably feel the same way, which is understandable. That said, it's simply human nature for some to goof off, complain, get snarky with peers, and otherwise behave like kids. The trick is to be a firm figure of authority that your team will respect. That's very important. If they don't respect you, they'll try to eat you alive, and they might even succeed. You gain respect when you set an example for others to follow and when you deal swiftly, fairly, articulately, sensitively, and firmly with any minor or major discipline problems that arise in the ranks.

Naturally, the seriousness and frequency of rule violations will dictate the specific approach and level of discipline required to address the offending employee. For example, some serious first-time infractions may dictate immediate discharge of employment; these might include selling or using illegal drugs while on the job, sexual harassment or physical assaults, verbal threats of violence, and the theft of valuable company property.

Some minor first-time offenses may simply call for an informal discussion or a written warning. Short of a firing, if your first formal counseling or disciplinary action did not work with an employee, then you would progress to the next appropriate counseling/disciplinary action step. In most cases, you would have been spelled out the next step in your previous warning notice. Generally speaking, three somewhat serious infractions and subsequent written warnings for the same type of behavior within a twelve-month period would result in termination.

Progressive counseling: Not every employee requires progressive discipline—a series of disciplinary meetings combined with written warnings that spell out the infraction and the consequences of continued similar behavior. But some may nevertheless require your attention, along with progressive counseling. These are the individuals who seem to be having trouble carrying out their duties for whatever reason but who do not exhibit behavior that demands disciplinary action from you. In some ways, employees like this are harder to deal with than the ones who behave badly. After all, a violation of company policy or procedure is clearly defined, as are the penalties, whereas a fellow human being trying his or her best and coming up short represents a sort of mystery begging to be solved. It also represents a drain on company resources, a threat to efficiency, and a risk to you personally as a manager because your department or business unit is bound to suffer if you have a weak link in the chain. Your superiors will notice, and they'll want to know what's going on.

You can draw several conclusions when certain employees are struggling to perform the jobs they were hired or promoted to carry out, or if the strugglers have suddenly found themselves in a job that was modified to meet current business needs, and they just don't seem to know what to do. The cause of the trouble may stem from a lack of proper training and/or the necessary aptitude, ability, or skills to perform their jobs. The cause could also simply be that they are lazy and possess a poor work ethic. It's up to you to find out—to solve the mystery, as it were—and to take the appropriate corrective action.

Coping with these types of employee deficiencies will require additional patience and effort from you and your team. Chances are, you noticed the problems for a reason. The assigned tasks of these employees were most likely not being completed in a timely fashion, and errors were probably being made with enough frequency to start impacting customers and/or product quality. As a consequence, the rest of your team would have had to work harder than ever to deliver a decreasing level of performance. Another downside when these issues crop up is that you or someone on your team will have to spend extra time to do progressive counseling. And if you are not successful in helping an employee correct the problems through coaching and/ or training, you will be forced to fire him or her. Then you'll have to go through the often painful and time-consuming process of hiring and training new employees.

It's no wonder then that many managers simply look at a poorly performing employee and exercise the shortcut solution of firing him or her. Progressive counseling can take a lot of time, but I think it's worth doing for many reasons. The first step is to identify the deficiency (what's important to you but is not being achieved up to your expectations). Meet with the employee to discuss your concerns and to fully identify the root cause of the problem. It's worth remembering that things are not always as they appear and that the employee may have a very good explanation for what is happening. The solution may be easy too, but don't count on it. Odds are the employee will have no idea that you are displeased until you both sit down for the meeting.

On the other hand, you may discover that the employee recognizes that he or she is not qualified for the job and elects to resign. You may learn that the employee has not yet received adequate training or proper instructions on what is expected. If the performance concern appears to be a training issue, then you'll need to implement an appropriate training program. In the event that your meeting results in no new revelations to help explain the employee's poor performance, then simply reiterate your concerns and thoroughly communicate your minimum standards and expectations for each task.

As you conclude your meeting, be sure to talk about what the consequences might be should the employee not achieve the minimum improvements you're looking for, but do it nicely. The employee is already going to feel bad, insecure, and maybe browbeaten. Set specific follow-up dates to discuss the employee's progress. Offer encouragement. Motivate the employee to do better. Without fail, you need to document in writing a summary of what was discussed in all formal counseling sessions. Ditto for disciplinary meetings.

Failure to document counseling or disciplinary sessions in writing will make it difficult to demonstrate that proper and adequate work performance or behavior concerns and warnings were given to the employee. It doesn't matter what format you use for this purpose as long as you get the facts on paper and signed by the advised employee to acknowledge receipt of the document. I prefer using a memo-style format for most situations involving managers. And typically I use a more structured preprinted form for non-management personnel. You can find a sample of both formats in Appendix A.

Employees with work-performance deficiencies should be progressively counseled (coached and trained, if necessary) over a period of thirty to ninety days. The employee's work performance should improve to meet your minimum standards and expectations during this period. If it does not, and it's clear that the person lacks the skills and abilities to perform the job, then you have no choice but to terminate employment, subject to your company's policies and any existing labor contracts and/or labor laws that may come into play.

Tips in a Nutshell

- Knowing federal and state labor laws and following your company's standard procedures for disciplining and firing personnel will help prevent costly lawsuits.
- Good managers must occasionally fire employees, but you should look to yourself first to see if you're the problem.
- Nip disciplinary problems in the bud. Spell out—in writing—the consequences of continued bad behavior.

- Taking immediate action when an underperforming employee is identified will mitigate damage to your department or business unit.
- Progressive counseling is an important tool when trying to save an underperforming employee from termination.
- Too much turnover, excessive disciplinary problems, and a lack of efficiency in your department or business unit will hurt your standing with upper management.
- Termination should be considered a last resort.

6

Managing Your Team

A company is nothing more than a group of people banded together to offer a service or product in the marketplace to generate profit. That's what a business is at the most basic level, though of course we all know that a company is more than that. Much more. It is an entity unto itself, a player in the market, an innovator, an influencer, a bully, or an angel. Yet, a company truly is all about its people at a core level, and as a manager you cannot expect to achieve the objectives your boss has set for you without the concerted efforts of your team. People grease the wheels of business, and it's your job to make sure that your particular part of the company works like a well-oiled machine.

Being a good manager means motivating others to work hard to achieve a common objective.

Managing people isn't easy, but it's the most important part of your job. You'll deal with subordinates, members of other departments (bosses and underlings), your superiors, vendors, and customers. All of these people require some form of management. Naturally, the players on your immediate team will require most of your attention. We'll talk about a number of issues related to personnel and customers in the next several chapters. In this one, I want to touch on some broad issues related to managing your team that you'll need to think about as you begin working in your new management position.

The average manager supervises five to ten employees at one time, and without the full support and cooperation of your team, you will likely struggle and fail. Your bosses will quickly notice that you aren't an effective leader, and so will everyone who works for you. From there, it all goes downhill fast. Suddenly, you're facing slumping performance across the entire spectrum of your department, lax discipline, and a loss of control.

Every manager wonders (or should wonder) how to best utilize the skills and talents of every employee and how to create a work culture that encourages and rewards the full, efficient, and cooperative efforts of each and every employee 100 percent of the time, even when the manager is out of the office and at the beach for a week. Managing people will test your administrative and leadership abilities, and the challenges will continue for as long as you remain in management. That's simply the nature of the beast, and if you don't feel comfortable with that, then you might want to consider doing something else. The following points will help you ensure that your team is as happy and as motivated as possible. A happy team is an effective team!

Talent counts.

Surround yourself with very talented people, but love the lifers too. Strive for a balanced mix of both superstar employees and employees I call lifers. A lifer is perfectly content with his or her current job duties; and in some cases promotion isn't an option because the employee has risen as far as possible within the company.

Unless your organization offers unlimited career growth opportunities, top-performing employees will eventually get restless and move on if they are not promoted within a reasonable time frame. This could lead to high employee turnover if not managed properly. On the other hand, lifers are good, reliable employees who are happy with their current jobs and have little or no ambition for advancement. They are long-term employees who possess a wealth of company knowledge that will help provide operating stability when the business does experience employee turnover. Lifers have talent too, and it is wise to treat them with the respect they deserve. No company can run well with a staff comprised solely of either superstars or lifers. As I've said, you need a mix of both.

Communication matters.

Hold regularly scheduled staff meetings. Although I spent time talking about this already, I think another paragraph to drive home the importance of the subject is in order, so here goes! As a manager, you are responsible for making sure that your people know what is expected of them and that they have the proper tools to get their jobs done. You can't do your job if you're not talking with your team. Encourage a culture of openness in which your people feel like they can ask questions, offer suggestions, and compare notes in their ongoing effort to accomplish the objectives you have set for the team. The monthly staff meeting is an excellent venue for dialogue.

Be accessible. Make it easy for your team to connect with you. Routinely get out from behind your desk and wander around your areas of accountability. It's your job to understand what is going on in the trenches (the good and bad), and to do that you need to ask questions. A staff meeting is an excellent venue for that, but don't wait for a monthly meeting. It's important for you to be accessible at all times. I usually pose the same question to many different people when trying to get a true assessment of a given situation. I ask employees if they are enjoying their work and if they have ideas that might help make them more efficient and effective at their jobs. You'll be astonished at what you can learn when you go out and kick the tires and look under the hood of your organization.

If you hibernate in your office and make yourself difficult to reach, you become disconnected from what's going on behind the scenes of your business. You send the message to your employees that you are disinterested in what's important to them. They in turn become apathetic about their jobs, further removing you from what is really happening in your business unit. Don't rely solely on the filtered information from one or two of your direct reports to learn what may or may not be going on outside your office. You need to get out and mingle with your team to learn firsthand what the facts are.

Typically, managers who hide and seclude themselves rely too heavily on internal data, written reports, and other people for operational, personnel, and general information feedback. Relying too much on one or two individuals can be problematic. These employees will sometimes skew or spin the information to suit their personal agendas, or they'll communicate what they think you want to hear. These people might be disingenuous or incompetent, or they may have no clue about how to interpret current business conditions.

Either way, as the manager in charge you certainly don't want to rely solely on the thoughts of one or two information feeders. After all, most people would not purchase a home or a car sight unseen and solely on the advice of a friend, home inspector, or the local auto mechanic. Would you? I didn't think so. If you're like most people, you'll likely want to get out and personally view and inspect the home or car (like checking under the hood and test driving the vehicle) prior to making a final decision to buy.

Likewise, a business is very much like your favorite automobile. It will give you many years of reliable service and value, assuming you don't neglect it. Like your car, your business requires frequent checks, inspections, and tune-ups (a little TLC). You sometimes have to replace parts in a car, and unfortunately, you have to sometimes replace employees in a business to keep them both running as designed.

Don't shoot your mouth off. Be careful about what you say, and be cautious about who you're talking to. You don't want to say something to an employee that you're not willing to see posted all over the Internet, and this becomes especially important as you climb farther up the corporate ladder. When hourly employees engage in unprofessional chitchat, it can be considered gossip, something I firmly discourage anytime I hear it. When managers do it, however, that's even worse. Your words and actions can quickly escalate to a scandalous level, hampering your ability to effectively manage your team.

You can't do it all.

Master the art of delegation. Obviously, you can't do everything to make your business unit a success, even if it's tempting to try. Face it. We managers tend to be Type A overachievers, and we nurse the notion that we can do the job at hand better than anyone else. That's natural, but it's also dangerous and often untrue anyway. The key to management excellence lies in delegating tasks to the right people on your team, matching skill sets with assignments to get the desired results. Think about it. If you continually perform the tasks your employees should be performing, you squander valuable time that would be best utilized managing your business. After all, that's why you were hired.

Do not act as the automatic backup or the do-over person for your subordinates when they fall behind in their work or continually fail to perform their jobs to the level of the prescribed minimum standards and expectations. For example, do not take on tasks simply because you believe it will be easier for you to "just do it" rather than take the time to train and coach your employees on how to correctly perform their duties. While it may very well be easier for you to do a particular job and resolve an issue in the short term, the fact is that the overriding problem will remain. Your team members will never learn to do their jobs correctly and efficiently if you continue to bail them out.

In addition, employees may come to realize they don't have to raise their standards and productivity if you and others routinely step in to perform their work. Failing to nip this issue in the bud early on will result in your wasting an enormous amount of time over the long term, and that will limit your ability to grow professionally. If you are not managing your business, then nobody is. Most likely the business is actually managing you.

Avoid the task trap. The task-trap concept is very closely related to the importance of delegating. If you don't delegate, you'll fall into the task trap, and that's a bad thing. Every hour that you perform a task for a subordinate is an hour that you're not managing your department or business. You're not reviewing business performance reports, coaching and training team members, inspecting operations, or providing management oversight, and you're not focused on improving company strategies, production, service, and so on. Falling into the task trap can lead to poor results that your superiors will notice, and that can torpedo your career.

At the end of each day at the office, think back to everything you did while you were there, and identify the tasks you could have and should have delegated to a staff member. Then make appropriate adjustments in your priorities going forward.

Get the job done right and on time.

Your staff should be dedicated to meeting deadlines. As I've said before, deadlines are important. Your department would grind to a halt without them. From the outset, establish a culture in your unit that encourages and rewards getting simple routine assignments done in seventy-two hours or less while maintaining the expected quality of the work. Sometimes, a scheduling conflict will get in the way, or a given project might require more time than originally thought, but for the most part, most deadlines should be held as nearly sacred. If you promise a customer or your superior that he or she will receive your work on a given day, failing to do so sends the message that you are either unorganized or inefficient, or that you don't care about the other person or the company.

All projects are top priority. Firmly but cheerfully communicating that all projects are top priority will help establish a near-zero tolerance for employees who say they're too busy to get everything done. As a manager, you will no doubt get that excuse from time to time. Talk with the employee to get a full understanding of why he or she is unable to meet routine deadlines. Sometimes there's a legitimate reason. At other times the employee is just not cut out for his or her job; or even worse, the individual in question is just lazy and not a team player. You'll quickly learn who those employees are.

Ensure that all documents are date stamped or reflect revision dates. You'll find that creating a culture in which all documents contain a creation or revision date (date stamp) will help everyone because your team won't mistakenly use old out-of-date documents. Each member of your team will be on the same page, and you will avoid costly or embarrassing situations.

Problems always crop up.

After scrambling to extinguish a fire, remember to find out what started it in the first place. Determining the root causes of a problem and putting a plan in place to make sure it doesn't happen again are essential components of a manager's role. As you go about your job, instill in your team the notion that solving a problem is only the first step. The next step is taking the time to understand why the problem cropped up at all and then implementing a plan to reduce the likelihood that the same thing might occur in the future. If you neglect the second step, you and members of your team will spend all of your time putting out what I call preventable fires.

It's worth noting that the above is a very easy management concept to implement. However, it does require situational awareness, discipline, perseverance, and adequate management oversight to successfully execute and maintain over the long term. Similarly, members of your team must act as ambassadors for your organization. They must possess diplomatic skills, and they must know how to effectively resolve routine and difficult customer service complaints, concerns, and requests.

Deal with the big problems first. Make sure you get your priorities in the proper order. I cannot tell you how often I see managers dealing with a relatively unimportant operating issue while a major fire rages on in another area of his or her business unit. The last thing you want to be is the proverbial captain of the *Titanic* who worries about the positioning of the deck chairs after your ship has hit an iceberg.

To carry on with the ship metaphor a little longer, remember that an aircraft carrier cannot turn around on a dime, nor can a sizable company in need of a major overhaul. Be patient, but also be methodical and relentless in pursuing your goals and objectives. It can take up to two years or more to successfully turn around a large and ailing company.

Plan for stormy weather. A company will occasionally encounter periods of difficulty. Markets can shift unexpectedly. A shakeup can occur in upper management. A supply chain can be temporarily interrupted. Employee turnover can spike. A good manager will quickly assess the situation and help the team navigate to calmer waters. An astute manager will have factored predictable problems into an effective business management design, preparing him or her to respond should the need arise.

Keep your perspective. When evaluating operating issues and searching for appropriate solutions, you do not want to reinvent the wheel or rewrite your entire playbook just because you encounter a rare event that adversely impacts your department and/or company. Stay cool and think things through. If you need to respond, then do so with a measured course of action that makes sense without overdoing it. You certainly wouldn't use an elephant gun to kill a fly, and you wouldn't use a fly swatter to take out an elephant.

Take the time you need to fully evaluate the seriousness and potential frequency of an issue before deciding on an appropriate plan. Allocate and balance your efforts and resources accordingly. As you address problems, remember to seek short- and long-term solutions and get at the root causes of the trouble.

Know when to actively manage and when to back off.

Get rid of the deadwood. Do not tolerate poorly performing employees. Imagine the worst person who has ever worked for you, or whom you've ever worked with. Now consider how long your current company would survive if all its employees performed at that same subpar level. I doubt the business would last long.

Bad employees can be walking disasters, and you don't want them around because they negatively impact customer service, operating efficiencies, and employee morale. You have a responsibility and a duty to terminate the employment of underperforming employees if you are unable to coach them to an acceptable work standard within a reasonable period of time.

Do not dumb down the job to an employee's capabilities or standards. It's essential to hold everyone accountable to the minimum performance standards you established at the outset.

Avoid micromanaging. Balance your efforts to provide adequate support and management oversight to your subordinates without crossing the line into micromanaging them. You do not want to dictate how your people arrange the items on their desks or what color shoes they wear throughout the week. However, you are responsible for the quality and quantity of work that your team produces, so by all means get out from behind the desk, kick those tires, and routinely take your business out for a test drive. Do not be afraid to occasionally ask your employees if they feel they need more or less support from you.

Pick your battles. You will not always agree with the opinions of others on your team regardless of their rank. Just should know that as a skillful manager you need not always have it your way. It is sometimes best to simply let some things go and reserve your opinions for the matters that are really important to you and your department.

Keep reprimands private. Always support your employees when in a public environment, even if you're ready to terminate an individual. In a way, you are like a parent, so you don't want to show favoritism or make employees feel like you're picking on them. When it all comes down to it, you're the responsible adult in the room. All employee coaching, counseling, and reprimanding should be done in private behind closed doors. Managers sometimes wrongly berate employees in front of their peers without considering the consequences of doing so. This behavior is unprofessional; it's a morale buster for the entire team, and in some cases it could expose you and your company to lawsuits.

Project optimism, even if you're feeling pessimistic. Always maintain an optimistic attitude when in the presence of your team. You are the head cheerleader and coach. Your glass should always be half full, if not overflowing, with a can-do approach to daily routines, long-term strategic planning, and goal setting. Lead your team by example and don't forget to inject a little humor into the workplace. Employees will be more productive, efficient, and happier working in an environment they enjoy. Patting employees on the back, especially in front of their peers, is a good idea if you don't overdo it or play favorites. Everybody likes to be appreciated for a job well done.

Trust, but verify. Do not blindly sign off on employee time cards and product invoices. Time cards are like product and service provider invoices, and these invoices need to be scrutinized for accuracy. Consider employees as individual contractors who happen to be on your payroll. Make sure you are paying the correct number of straight, overtime, vacation, and sick-time hours each week.

Likewise, pay close attention to vender invoices. Ensure that the quantity, price, and quality of the items received are correct and consistent with what you ordered.

Tips in a Nutshell

- A good manager motivates the team to work together to accomplish company goals. Communicate your vision (it's not a secret), give team members the tools they need, and instill a can-do attitude in all of your people.
- Talented employees make achieving your objectives possible, whereas poor-performing employees drag you and the team down. Cultivate the lifers on your staff. They're just as important as superstars.
- Being accessible to your team makes it easier to head off large and small problems.
- Delegate all the tasks you can so you can focus on managing. Remember that you can't do everything.
- Make it clear to the team that every job or task is a priority. Deadlines should be met consistently.
- Plan for problems that will inevitably arise, and deal with the most serious ones first. Stay calm, cool, and collected as you devise a measured response to each issue. Solutions should include long-term preventive planning.
- Always project optimism in front of your team.

7

Managing Your Sales Staff

Modern societies around the globe are built around buying and selling, and it has been that way since civilization first took root in the Neolithic period when shells or other valuables were traded for goods. Money began to replace bartering in Mesopotamia back around 3,000 BCE, and it has played a part in the growth and decline of nations ever since. Think about it: The quest for spices led to the Age of Exploration and the search for the elusive Northwest Passage, all because nations wanted a slice of the profits from the spice trade. The search for riches led to territorial conquests and dark times, robust growth and financial busts. It also led to bloody wars, but that's another story.

We're in the same situation now, of course. The world is selling as usual, or trying to, and some of us are still buying, or trying to. When people are buying, times are good. When the money stops flowing, well, then we're in a bit of a bind because fewer people buy what is being sold, and that includes the products or services we're trying to sell. The latest economic calamity that started in 2008 amply demonstrates what happens when money supplies dry up and people can't buy or sell. My point is that sales of one kind or another occupy virtually every aspect of our lives whether we like it or not. This is especially true for you in your new job.

As a manager, you're selling all the time. I'm not talking about direct sales to customers, at least not yet. I'll get to that in much more detail a little later. I'm talking about selling yourself and your ideas to your team, your peers in other departments, and your bosses. Every initiative you put forth, every management plan you implement (or try to implement), and every motivational talk you give to your team members to get them to work harder and smarter represents a sort of sales campaign. It's important for you to view sales from this broad perspective. If you do, you'll see that acquiring knowledge and skills in sales of all kinds can only help you climb the corporate ladder to upper management, and presumably that's what you want, right?

A working knowledge of sales and marketing basics is an essential part of your job as a manager.

Understanding how your company actually generates business is part of your job too. You sell yourself and your ideas virtually every day, but you must also be cognizant of the efforts that go into selling the product or service your company provides for the customer. Even if you have nothing to do with the sales and marketing department, you need to be aware.

Let's take the finance department as an example. Processing payroll, managing accounts payable, and following through on the timely clearing of accounts receivable might not seem like it's related much to sales and marketing, but it is. For one thing, without sales and marketing, the finance department would have nothing to do, and neither would you! Crunching numbers to determine gross revenue, supply chain cost trends (cost of goods), net revenue, operating expenses and so on are all the result of sales and marketing efforts to generate business.

You might not think you need to care about sales and marketing if you work in finance, but you do. You should be aware of it, at least, and you should do what you can to support your peers who work in sales and marketing. Hopefully, they're doing a good job. One way to tell is to determine if advertising dollars spent are generating an effective return on the investment in terms of sales. What is the margin on that sale from a sales and marketing perspective? In other words, how much did the company have to spend in sales and marketing dollars to generate the sale, and then how much did it cost to make or purchase the product? As you can see, a business is organic in nature. Every part is connected, like number-crunching accounting managers in finance.

If you work in management for a restaurant, a hotel, a supermarket, a department store, an auto parts supply shop, a florist, or any other business operating at a local level, you'll be involved in sales and marketing. Customers will show up with coupons, print ads, Internet offers, and other promotional deals, and you will need to know which ones apply and which ones don't. In short, you will be indirectly involved in fulfilling the sales through good customer service.

You also might receive zillions of annoying cold calls from ad reps trying to sell you space in print or on the Internet, depending on the scope of your management duties and the size of your business. For example, a manager in a local store of a national burger chain isn't going to have to plan sales, marketing, and advertising programs to generate revenue, unless he or she owns the franchise. However, if you manage your own small business, you'll definitely get cold calls of this sort, and you'll definitely be fashioning your own integrated marketing, sales, and advertising campaigns that will most likely make or break the enterprise in terms of profitability. You will need to study the subject in far more depth than this book is meant to get into. Suffice it to say, efforts to generate revenue through sales, marketing, and advertising impact every aspect of a company large or small, and as a manager the results of those efforts are going to impact you.

A large number of new managers find themselves supervising sales staff.

It's a fact of life that most entry-level management jobs focus on sales of some kind. If you're promoted from flipping burgers to managing the store, you're going to focus on sales and customer service in a big way. That means managing your sales staff. If you were selling plumbing hardware as an outside salesperson and got promoted to the position of regional manager, then you'd have to manage people working in your former position. Name the most common first management jobs, and I can pretty much guarantee that supervising a sales staff or customer service folks will be front and center in the job description. Exceptions are in product design, research and development, computer programming, accounting, business administration, and other positions that support the company's effort to provide a service or product for its customers.

Chances are, you will inherit an existing sales program and staff. That can be good because you'll have a foundation to work upon. That can also be bad because the program might be flawed, and your employees will have gotten used to selling in a manner that might not be as conducive to overcoming customer objections, pointing out solutions to customer problems, and subsequently closing the sale. You'll need to take a good look at the program that's in place to see if you can make improvements. If any improvements are required, you'll need to work tactfully with your immediate supervisors and with your team to implement them.

Analyze the existing sales program to find its strengths and weaknesses.

Your first step in your new position is to know your product or service inside and out, and to know what your bosses expect of you. Get to know your staff, and ask lots of questions. Get feedback on what works and what doesn't. Then take a good hard look at your competitors. What do they excel at, and what are their weaknesses? If you spot any weaknesses, like in customer service, for example, try to figure out a way to exploit those weaknesses within the context of a positive sales approach that puts your company up as a worthy option for customers to consider. If you can, determine which competitor holds the most market share and then determine why. Is that competitor better at customer service than your company is? Are its products or services better? Does it have a better marketing, sales, and advertising program? Is it a matter of price? Make notes as you discover the answers to these questions.

After gathering the above information, you can begin to design a plan for success. I typically start off by assessing our current staff. Do we have the right personnel assigned to the correct tasks? You would not cast a sixty-year-old, overweight, gray-haired guy to perform as a young teenage heartthrob in a movie, would you? Of course not. Nor should you hire a professionally trained truck driver (who wants to be a truck driver) for a route sales position. True route sales professionals are salespeople who sell product off their truck. They are not simply delivering presold orders; rather, they focus on selling their product lines. They are motivated by the hunt, the sale, and the commission dollars that come with making the sale. Truck drivers are motivated by the independence of the job and being their own bosses, and they're quite happy not to have sales quotas. They are thrilled to receive consistent and reliable paychecks each week.

Naturally, you're probably not managing route sales—but, hey, you never know! The point is that no matter what kind of sales staff you manage, the key to your success is casting the right people in the right jobs. You want to make sure your existing employees are competent, focused on success, and passionate about their work. You will probably discover that some are simply putting their time in for their weekly paychecks. Too often, a manager will hold on to an incompetent or miscast employee because the manager is too complacent or lazy to fix the problem. What these managers don't realize is that they will actually create many more challenges and much more work for themselves over the long term by not managing these personnel issues early on.

Surround yourself with the best, brightest, and most competent people you can find and that your budget will allow. You want people who truly love the jobs they are assigned to do and who are as passionate as you are about staying focused and getting their jobs done correctly as requested. If you have to make changes, add to your private notes the names of employees who might need remedial work prior to termination. Whatever you do, don't tell anyone that personnel changes may be in the offing. That will kill morale in a hurry, and your sales results will suffer. When the time comes, manage the problem employees as described in earlier chapters.

Even the best point-of-sale and support staff can benefit from ongoing training.

Once the correct sales and support personnel are in place, it's time to take a careful look at training and procedures. In my model, all support staff (anyone who may have an opportunity to interact with customers, such as the receptionist, backup personnel, and customer service representatives) must receive basic training about the products and services we offer. These employees need to have a working knowledge of our product line, as well as the entire process from ordering through delivery, and they must be fully trained to overcome the most frequent and difficult sales objections they may encounter from our customers. Sadly, that's sometimes easier said than done, but good managers can accomplish the objectives.

Customers walking in your door or calling to inquire about your company's services or products are often rushed. They want basic information at the time of the initial request, not necessarily the next day. Don't you hate it when you don't get the answers to basic questions right away? Well, your customers do too. If the processes in place in your sales program delay providing information, find out why to see if the problem can be addressed. Some programs are set up so that the prospect must meet with a sales rep before answers can be given. In my book, that's a recipe for losing sales. The prospects do not always have the time or the interest to meet with a sales rep on the initial inquiry.

You do not want to lose potential buyers because of the ignorance of frontline personnel. These point-of-sale staffers require the basic knowledge needed to answer prospects' questions and motivate them. The staffers also need to project competence and a sincere appreciation for customers' interest in your products or services. Can you imagine a company investing heavily in putting together the best sales and marketing team money could buy, yet continually failing to convert an acceptable number of incoming leads into sales? It happens all the time. Managers invest large amounts of time, money, and energy developing an outstanding sales organization that generates above-average leads, and then totally disregard the quality of work delivered by their point-of-sale and other support personnel. As you analyze your existing sales program and staff, take a good look at the level of training that the people supporting your sales team receive. And don't get cheap or lazy when it comes to fully training your frontline team. Your whole organization is relying on you to make this happen.

Following up on all inquiries and qualified leads in a timely manner will maximize your return on marketing and advertising dollars.

It's also essential in your early analysis of your existing sales program to make sure you have a process in place to follow up on all inquiries in a timely manner. In my opinion, a live person should answer all incoming phone calls. If that's not possible, then phone and Internet sales inquiries should be followed up on within four hours (two is better).

Establish an eighteen-hour minimum standard for inquiry follow-ups; this should not be a difficult task for most companies to achieve. Ideally, all morning and early afternoon inquiries should be addressed on the same day they are received, and late-afternoon queries should be acknowledged and taken care of first thing the next morning. However, if your company does business with firms that rely on your products or services to keep functioning, you'll obviously have to cut down your response time to provide nearly instantaneous responses to calls. Say a local restaurant's soda system goes down during the lunch hour. The owner calls you (their service provider) for service, but you don't respond until the next day. You'd be mighty angry if you were the restaurant owner, and you'd probably fire any company that treated you like that.

Winning companies offer superior services or products at a great value, and they outperform their competitors in customer service. Their marketing, sales, and advertising programs are typically well organized, creative, innovative, well funded, and staffed with professionals dedicated to carrying out the mission of turning inquiries and leads into sales. In addition to establishing a timely system for following through with inquiries, does your program include a simple and methodical process for sales reps to follow up with those customers who do not buy on their initial contact with your company? You want to maximize the sales potential of each and every lead. Assume you can convert every lead over time.

Does your program include a procedure whereby sales reps follow up with new and longtime customers for the purpose of up-selling products and services or obtaining new customer leads from these clients? This particular group will be your best advocates and business promoters if their experiences with your company have been superb and your service has been exemplary. Does your program include a referral incentive whereby current customers who recommend your products and services to friends and relatives can then receive some sort of monetary reward in appreciation?

You may be surprised to find that your inherited sales program does not include minimum performance standards documents or fully developed job descriptions. If you lack these vital documents, create and integrate them into your program. Everyone on your team must know what is expected.

Remember, business breeds business. If a company leads the industry in customer service standards and provides a high-quality product or service at an excellent perceived value, that's a recipe for success. If your sales team is working for such a company, you're already well on your way to personal fulfillment and financial rewards as a newly hired manager.

True sales professionals are difficult to find, and they are sometimes difficult to keep.

Sales work is tough. How would you like going up to complete strangers and asking them to buy something from you? Maybe you'd be fine with that. In fact, if you are managing a sales staff, I hope you are! But the truth is, most of us hate the idea of selling something. It goes against our nature. If you have excellent salespeople on your team already, then be grateful. You'll be doubly glad you gave significant attention to ensuring that frontline staff was trained to fully support your sales team and provide outstanding customer service to existing customers.

If you have doubts about the efficiency and quality of your existing sales staff, you have to take an objective look and consider what to do next. Leave any doubtful employees in place while you figure out your next step. Just don't take too long to make your move. In the initial phases of getting to know your team, find out just how much members know about all company products, services, policies, and procedures. You might be surprised at the knowledge gaps you unearth. Don't immediately lean to the termination option if you do. Remember, firing can be expensive for many reasons, and it can really kick you in the rear if the word gets around to your superiors that you're heavy on the ax without making your position crystal clear. Retraining and coaching are frequently the best options.

I look for the following in my sales team:

- Members must fully understand—and be able to effectively communicate to our customers—the benefits and added value of purchasing our products and doing business with our company.

- Members must be fully knowledgeable and effective in placing product orders and must possess the knowledge to answer routine customer service questions without having to rely on others.

- Members must learn the value of identifying what's important to the customer, something I like to call the art of discovery. Often, the discovery is identifying the objection to the sale or a solution to the customer's problems. Is the customer ready, willing, and able to buy? If he or she is, but still isn't buying, it's the salesperson's job to find out why.

- Members must become conscious of their own personality traits and then use that knowledge to identify the behavioral qualities of others. Personality profile tests can help.

- Members must bond with and sell themselves to potential customers.

- Members must be entirely capable of addressing the most frequent and difficult sales objections that buyers might raise about your product and services during a sales presentation. Overcoming objections leads to closed sales—that cannot be emphasized enough.

- Members must be good closers. They've got to ask for the sale.

After basic training, sales personnel will be required to "mystery shop" our key competitors and learn firsthand what they excel at and where their weak points are. They need to see and experience what customers experience when visiting our competitors. This information will be enormously useful when a potential buyer references a competitor during the sales process, and it will help sales staff to critique and perfect their own sales presentations. We want to learn and incorporate the best practices of other successful companies.

As part of the ongoing training process, I conduct role-playing sessions with sales personnel. The goal here is to practice various sales techniques and test the knowledge of the sales team. This exercise helps to build confidence, and it identifies areas in need of follow-up training. Buyers like doing business with thoroughly knowledgeable salespeople that are confident, personable, and able to identify with their needs. You will find that this is especially true of savvy buyers that prefer working with salespeople who are also capable of discussing the dynamics of the industry and its major competitors.

Identifying the source and costs of your sales leads is important in any sales effort.

If you're part of a larger organization; the management of marketing and advertising will be separate, though you and your bosses will work hand-in-hand with your peers in those sister departments to generate leads and subsequent profits. If you are a sales manager for a smaller company, you might very well be asked to wear multiple hats.

Regardless of the size of the business you're working in, the goal is to make as many people as possible aware of your company, its products or services, and the excellent reputation it enjoys in the marketplace. More exposure often translates into more sales, though not always. Business is a numbers game. The company with the best integrated marketing, sales, and advertising campaign will be the one most likely to capture the greatest share of the market. The size of the company and the entire marketing, sales, and advertising budget also factor into the equation.

A big challenge is determining which advertising and marketing expenditures generate the most productive sales leads, and that challenge cuts across businesses of all sizes and kinds. In order to make that determination, you first have to know the sources of your leads and referrals. This can be accomplished in many different ways, such as by assigning an identifying phone number to each lead source category. Or, you can simply have sales and point-of-sale personnel ask the question during sales presentations and inquiries. Retailers often ask for your zip code or some other piece of identifying information when you're cashing out because they're trying to track their marketing and advertising leads. They want to see what advertising is working (or not) and use that information to refine where to target their future advertising dollars.

The next step is identifying the source of your most productive leads. Differentiating between advertising vehicles that produce few leads and those that produce lots of leads is a basic requirement in marketing. However, identifying which vehicle produces the most sales and product orders as compared to the total number of leads received is very important. For example, an ad that produces one hundred leads with a 20 percent sales conversion rate would be considered a much better value than an ad that produced one hundred leads with only a 5 percent sales conversion rate. The above assumes that each ad cost the same amount.

A Florida Scenario

At times, providing an actual scenario can better illustrate a point. The story below is based on the challenges of marketing real estate in Florida.

A large segment of senior citizens living in Florida no longer want to live in neighborhoods full of kids. To fill that market niche, many developers built what are known as active adult communities restricted to people ages fifty-five and up. Amenities, activity directors, lots of golf, swimming pools, and other features are usually part of active adult communities and represent a major draw. Other active adult communities are more modest and cater to less affluent homebuyers, but the concept remains the same.

Now let's assume you own a community for people fifty-five and up. The homes are manufactured residences in a community located in central Florida. To take advantage of the upcoming busy tourist season, which brings visitors to Florida in search of some winter warmth, you decide to run an ad campaign for your home sales department in January. Your sales promotion includes placing an ad for your homes on a large billboard just outside your community along a heavily traveled tourist route. You also decide to place similar ads in the employee newsletters of all the major theme parks.

At the end of the month, you analyze the data and learn that you received one hundred inquiries from the theme park ads, which resulted in five home sales. Most of these leads came in via phone and your website, with only a handful of walk-in traffic to your sales office. Further analysis indicates that most of the inquiries from the theme park ads were from prospects who weren't fifty-five years old and who therefore could not buy in the community you were selling. These buyers were ready, willing, and able to purchase a home, but they were terrible leads because they couldn't buy because of the age restriction. Thus, the number of qualified buyers from that pool of prospects was very low, accounting for the low sales conversion rate.

The billboard, however, generated one hundred leads as well, but it produced twenty home sales. The demographics of these leads were much different. The majority came from the gray-haired crowd who happened to be wintering in Florida and who happened to have an interest in buying homes for permanent residency. Most of these customers simply walked into the sales office after seeing the billboard. While there were a few phone inquiries, there were no website requests for information from this ad. And because each ad vehicle cost one thousand dollars, clearly the best value for your advertising dollars was the billboard ad. The billboard delivered prospects who were more qualified.

The table below shows the respective costs and results.

	Ad Costs	Leads	Lead Cost	Home Sales	Lead Cost per Sale
Billboard ad:	$1,000	100	$10	20	$ 50
Theme park ads:	$1,000	100	$10	5	$200

Fully analyzing the data provides a good view of the effectiveness of your marketing programs. You will obtain valuable information to help you identify where and how to best invest your advertising and marketing dollars going forward. As a new sales manager in a larger company, you may not be in on analyses like this one, but you will be someday. And if you're a new business owner or the new sales manager in a smaller firm, you'll be taking the plunge into this arena right away. Track and qualify the leads and then target the marketing and advertising vehicles that produce the most qualified potential buyers.

Counting costs matters.

Consider calculating what your average lead costs are each month relative to your company's total fixed operating costs. Share this information with appropriate sales personnel; it can be a great motivating tool.

Here's an example: Your average monthly operating costs (as reflected on your profit and loss statement) are twenty thousand dollars. You typically receive fifty leads per month. That means your average overhead cost per lead is four hundred dollars. The theory here is that it takes the entire team and all the associated operating expenses to produce and support incoming leads through the entire sales process. The only people paying for all this overhead and costs are your customers. Thus, while it's imperative to understand the actual costs for each lead your company brings in (and the best value for your advertising dollars), it is also important to understand the total operating costs associated with each lead and eventual sale.

If your sales staff knows the overhead costs attached to each lead, it might drive home the point that the sales presentation has a lot more riding on it than a commission. It represents a financial investment from the company on behalf of the salesperson. Sharing the information with frontline staff can similarly motivate them. At the very least, everyone on your team will know how much is on the line each time the phone rings and each time a salesperson gives a presentation.

Once you have evaluated the nature of your existing sales program and the quality of the staff you have inherited, methodically begin implementing any changes you deem necessary. Just be mindful that you are working with people, and that change often does not come easily. People despise change, in fact, or at least most of us do; so tread lightly but firmly in your quest to eliminate any deficiencies in your sales program and be sure to manage your staff all the way to the pinnacle of success for yourself and for them.

And when the team does well, don't hold back the praise. Superb performance should be rewarded with sales incentives, commissions, and/or bonuses as appropriate for your specific industry and as business conditions allow. Without sales and customers, nobody at your company would get a paycheck!

Tips in a Nutshell

- As a manager, you're selling yourself and your message all the time to your subordinates, peers, and bosses.
- Analyze the sales program you inherited and then refine it as necessary to maximize results.
- Get feedback from existing frontline and sales staff to identify knowledge gaps and inefficient procedures. Implement training programs and institute procedural changes to correct problems.
- Ensure that only top performers remain on your sales team.

- If necessary, create minimum performance standards documents and job descriptions. Make sure every member of your team knows what is expected of him or her.
- Track lead sources and costs associated with lead generation. Weed out underperforming marketing and advertising vehicles.

8

Managing Your Customers

It should be obvious to you by now in your role as a new manager that dealing with people in a variety of capacities will constitute the lion's share of your job. Clearly, properly managing your direct reports (employees) is vital. Functioning within the company's hierarchy is another key area where your skills with people will come into play, smoothing the way to success and promotions or blocking your progress up the ladder if you fail to work well with and motivate others. Your peers, immediate supervisors, and bosses in upper management all fit into your sphere of influence, as do your suppliers and vendors. In this service-oriented economy, chances are also good that part of your job will include interacting directly with customers, and/or managing employees who do.

A company is nothing without its customers. Without them, you don't get paid and you don't get promoted, something that's really important to remember when you are dealing with a difficult customer. Without an adequate level of customer service in place, companies will usually perform poorly and will sometimes fail. Of course, other deficiencies can take down a company, such as inferior products, a poor business management design, and operating inefficiencies that add unnecessary costs to doing business, thereby putting a drag on profits. All of these problems can harm the viability of a company. However, with all things being equal, the level of customer service offered by a business (especially when compared to its competitors) can have a profound negative or positive impact on a company's success.

It doesn't take a rocket scientist to figure these things out, but you'd be surprised at how often I've found that customer service is ignored or barely exercised. It frankly amazes me that some business owners do not go out of their way to ensure that high levels of customer care and service are in place and properly managed. But I've seen it time after time. I'm sure you've experienced lackluster or just plain bad customer service yourself, and I bet it really ticked you off. Bear that in mind as you go about managing your customers. Seeing them through the prism of your own bad experiences in the marketplace can (or should) instill in you an ardent desire to never annoy someone who is buying a product or service from your company.

Managers who are responsible for customer service employees need to understand how important these services are to the overall success of the business. I can't emphasize this enough. Customer service really matters. Just as important, you must recognize the awesome responsibility you have in ensuring your subordinates also understand that customer service is king and that if they are unsure of what to do in a tough situation regarding customer service they must come to you for guidance.

Excellent customer care matters as much as providing a quality product or service.

As you navigate your new position as a manager, consider that you actually have a set of three different types of customers, to use the term a bit broadly. I've mentioned them before, but let's spend time going into greater depth here. The essential point to remember is that, if you adopt a management approach that applies customer service concepts to every aspect of what you do, you'll stand a better chance of rising far in the company.

External customers: These are the most obvious of your customers. Simply put, any individual or entity that purchases your company's products or services is an external customer. I'll go into considerable detail on providing quality customer care for this all-important group.

Internal customers: In the broadest sense, this group includes anyone that you interact with who works for your company. An employee is an internal customer. So is your boss. So is the manager in a supporting department. You get the idea. If you think of this group as a pool of customers, you'll focus on providing quality customer service, just like you would for an external customer.

Third-party customers: Employees of companies that you rely on to support your business fall into this group. Your job will be much easier and more efficient if you treat your suppliers and vendors like important customers. You may be buying their services or products to make your business run well (so, in fact, you are their customer), but going out of your way to ensure that the relationship is good for both parties simply makes sense. Remember that a supplier or vendor can make you look good or bad in the eyes of your boss. Think about what would happen if you needed to make a product delivery deadline, and a vendor you annoyed held things up just to spite you. That kind of thing can and does go on.

External Customers

The nature of your business determines the type and number of external customers you have. A restaurant will have lots of customers. A small consulting company may only have a dozen or two top clients. Quality customer service is essential no matter what business you are in. A customer is a customer. It's that simple.

You probably would consider all activities carried out during verbal interactions between a customer and a company representative as the most common form of customer care and service, and you would be correct. Such interactions can be in person or via the telephone. They can arise from something as simple as a customer going to a burger store to order some food or from a more complex buying experience like hiring a real estate company to purchase a home. In these situations, everything a customer representative says to and does for the customer would be a form of customer care and service.

At the most basic level, you want to ensure that those of your subordinates who interact with external customers display professionalism and demonstrate proper social skills. In other words, they have to be polite. They have to know the products or services, and they have to understand and honor company policies and procedures. It's up to you to train and motivate them to want to serve every customer as efficiently as possible.

Ask yourself some basic questions about your employees. Is each customer representative dressed appropriately, smiling, and projecting a sincere appreciation for every customer's business? Is the rep utilizing professional phone etiquette? Is the rep adequately trained and knowledgeable about the company's products and services, and is he or she able to address customers' needs in a timely manner? Is the rep able to anticipate customers' needs and act accordingly? And does the rep thank each customer for his or her business? These are all examples of what you need for quality customer care.

Every industry, business, and marketplace is different in terms of what level of customer service is considered average or great. What may be unimportant to some customers can be very important to others. Make it your business to learn what the gold standards are for your industry and marketplace. Mystery shop your top competitors and learn what they do to earn such great customer service reputations (learn best practices wherever you can).

Talking with customers that you already have is also an excellent way to refine and improve your existing customer care practices. This goes back to the importance of communication. Find out if your current customer care is up to snuff with your competitors, and ask your customers if they are satisfied or if there are any areas that need improvement. Critique your own business through the eyes of your most critical customers, covering every angle and every possible customer experience. Then act on what you find out!

I would go a bit further than the basics and suggest that customer service also consists of everything a customer might experience as part of any business encounter he or she may have with a company. This would include all items and things that are under the direct control of a company that can influence the customer's overall buying experience.

The exterior of your store (curb appeal) speaks volumes about what one might find on the inside, and it begins the customer service experience. Is the parking lot clean, and is it well lit after sunset? Is the exterior of the building well maintained and appropriately decorated and identified, making it easy for your customers to find you? Is the inside of the building organized, clean, stocked, adequately illuminated, and marked with signs so that customers can find what they're looking for? Are the bathrooms clean and stocked at all times?

The above are all passive forms of customer service that contribute to or detract from the customer's overall buying experience with a company. As a manager, even if you or your subordinates aren't interacting directly with external customers, you need to be aware that you still can have a positive or negative impact on customer service. If you manage a warehouse, how well you run it affects how quickly people can find a product and get it to the shipping department. Take a few minutes to analyze your job. How do your duties indirectly impact customer service? You might be surprised to see that you do make a difference. Naturally, if you directly interact with external customers, then the importance of your role in providing quality customer service is obvious.

Every industry is different, but quality customer care shares one thing across industries—a satisfied person from start to finish in the transaction.

As I've said, quality customer service is essential. Without it, the company won't prosper and neither will you. A variety of customer services enhance the customer's buying experience before, during, and after the sale. Professionally addressing the concerns a customer may have during a business relationship with your company also contributes to overall customer satisfaction, or the lack of it. If you do it right, you'll set your company a notch above the competition. Happy customers will return to a company that, well, makes them happy! Happy customers will usually act as walking and talking billboards that promote their favorite stores among friends and relatives. People love to brag after they enjoy an above-average experience at a great value.

Think about cruise ship companies and other businesses in the leisure industry. These companies go to great lengths to please their customers because they want repeat business, and they also want the happy customers to promote their products and services to friends and relatives. That in turn helps the overall sales and marketing position of the company, and it helps to build a continuous demand for the services and products.

One last point: It generally does not cost a lot of money to provide a high level of customer care and service. It simply requires management time and commitment to ensure all employees are providing it as prescribed and expected. Remind your team that it's the customer who pays their wages and will ultimately provide the funding for their next pay raise, and when you do employee reviews make customer service a key performance indicator. Make sure everyone knows that customer service will be a significant factor in determining the level of merit pay increases for each employee.

A superior customer service program should include creating a minimum performance standards document.

To help implement an effective plan to ensure superior customer care is delivered consistently, I suggest you create a minimum performance standards document for all appropriate personnel to adhere to. Then provide the training, coaching, and adequate management oversight required to achieve and sustain this important objective.

I've included a sample minimum performance standards document in Appendix A, but to stay on the topic here for a little longer, let me just say that I recommend you include the following behaviors and qualities in the document you create. It doesn't take a genius to provide superior customer service, but it does take work.

- **Acknowledgement:** Make it a point to acknowledge and greet everyone you come into contact with.
- **Professionalism:** Be nice, polite, courteous, and well mannered at all times.

- **Enthusiasm:** Show some excitement and sincere interest in your customer's wants and needs.
- **Focus:** Do not allow yourself to be interrupted by outside distractions when working with customers. Do not disrupt others who may be working with customers.
- **Tolerance:** Be patient, especially when working with difficult customers. The ability to display calm and patience during difficult situations is a mark of professionalism.
- **Understanding:** Empathize with your customers. Understand their feelings and perspective when they share their concerns and issues with you.
- **Stay Informed:** Be fully knowledgeable about company policies, procedures, products, services, and current inventory levels, if applicable.
- **Team Player:** Remember to provide unconditional support to your internal customers when they request help that is appropriate for you to give.
- **Common Sense:** Common sense must always prevail.

Internal Customers

You may be wondering, "How can my fellow employees, peers, and bosses be my customers?" and "What kind of customer service would I provide?" Those are fair questions. In fact, I think it is highly likely that you have never considered using the word "customer" to describe these people, nor is it likely that you've thought that doing the best job you can at all times counted as delivering superior customer service to these people. But in all the important senses, that's exactly what you're doing.

In a Utopian environment, employees working to carry out the company's business would treat each other like external customers, jumping through reasonable hoops to meet their needs. This high level of employee cooperation would result in the most efficient and cooperative workplace in the world. Even the best companies don't run like that, but some achieve a better track record for this kind of cooperative corporate culture than others. Hopefully, your company is supportive. The practice of working to obtain the highest levels of unconditional employee cooperation is fundamental for every company's success. It's also worth noting that it's fundamental to your own success as well.

As you pursue your duties, lead your team by example and motivate every member to act as though everyone they interact with is an external customer. Where appropriate, encourage employees to proactively assist other team members after observing a need, and to volunteer to help others when the call goes out for assistance. Show appreciation for team members who offer or agree to train and mentor others, and who consistently treat their coworkers like external customers, demonstrating consistently high levels of customer care and respect.

Make it known that going above and beyond the usual call of duty in what employees do will get noticed and rewarded. Bear in mind that, as you lead by example, subordinates and your bosses will notice your efforts. Individual employees who proactively provide high levels of customer service to their internal customers will build reputations as customer service rock stars that will go a long way in furthering their careers. These same employees are more likely to receive reciprocal help in kind from their peers and their subordinates when the fur hits the fan. Remember that your peers and subordinates can go out of their way to help you, or they can gleefully watch as you crash and burn.

If your employees treat each other like external customers, there's less likelihood of office politics and gossip taking hold in your workplace. Both can be like cancers to a company. Do everything you can to eliminate and avoid these destructive behaviors. When one of your employees intentionally picks on a coworker or is simply uncooperative with others, privately tell the person that he or she is in violation of the desired corporate culture. Do it right away. Malcontents like that hamper your ability to manage your business. They are not working to help you or your team achieve the objectives you hired them to carry out. They are not working in the company's best interest, and they certainly are not working to make your job easier. Quite the opposite! Do not tolerate this type of behavior.

Third-Party Customers

It should be crystal clear that team work, cooperation, attention to detail, excellent people skills, a strong work ethic, and so much more all factor into someone becoming a highly successful manager. The idea that you would treat a supplier or vendor with professionalism and sensitivity might sound a little strange to some of you. You may be thinking, "Hey, I'm the external customer, not them! I'm paying their company for a product or service! I should be treated like royalty!"

That kind of attitude gets new managers in trouble all the time. They end up pissing off important suppliers and vendors, which can really mess these managers up down the road. Just because the company needs your business doesn't mean you can treat the people you work with at that company like servants. They are pros just like you, and they deserve respect. It's all about forging mutually beneficial business relationships and fostering a sense of cooperation. If warranted, be firm when voicing a concern or addressing a problem, but always maintain your professionalism.

Any reasonable efforts you make that will help your suppliers succeed in their own business endeavors will pay you dividends down the road. This can be as simple as acting as a reference if asked or referring business their way if it's appropriate to do so. Treat your suppliers like internal customers. Don't be afraid to jump through some hoops to assist them and respond to their reasonable requests. Return phone calls and reply to e-mails in a timely manner, and do whatever it takes to get the supplier or vendor paid on time.

You are trying to build a strong rapport and business relationship with your suppliers and vendors. You are your supplier's external customer, but remember that your third-party customer would appreciate the same business relationship with you that you're trying to build with your own external customers. The benefits can be equally rewarding, regardless of customer type. Your suppliers can be a great source of customer referrals for your business. This presupposes, of course, that your supplier believes you're a professional who will provide excellent customer care for anyone they refer, and that the goods or services you sell are of high quality and represent great value.

When you help your suppliers to be more successful and efficient, you are helping them to help you. This could be in the form of lower product and service costs to you. It's more likely that your third-party customer will go out of the way to offer you special assistance when the need arises.

Maintaining a professional disposition costs you virtually nothing, but this positive behavior can bring you many benefits when you least expect it.

Always keep your cool when dealing with problem customers.

We've all been on the receiving end of terrible customer service, and none of us likes it. I've noticed over the years that there is a general correlation in the quality of customer service a company provides and the number of competitors in the marketplace. For example, if a town has just one cable TV company, chances are good that the level of customer service is going to be pretty low. The presence of more competitors usually translates into better customer care, but not always. You'll also be more likely to receive better customer service at businesses that rely on high volume and repeat customers, and from small companies and individuals that rely on word-of-mouth referrals. Again, though, that's not always the case.

The biggest reason that companies of all sizes (regardless of industry) fail miserably at providing adequate customer care is that management doesn't make it a priority. It's that simple, and such a deficiency goes back to having a poor business management design. It also speaks to a glaring lack of competency in the management team. If you work at a company like that and interact with external customers, you're going to find yourself very busy dealing with lots of angry people. If your company has wonderful customer care practices, you'll still face the proverbial music sooner or later. The only good thing is that this will occur much less often.

Let's take a restaurant or retail store as an example of what will lead to customer complaints. If the staff is untrained and lacks adequate management oversight, frontline customer service people will provide the level of service they think is appropriate and that they feel like dispensing at any given time (this will vary widely with each individual). Customers will complain, and then it becomes your problem. In many cases, as with retail stores and restaurants, the frontline supervisors of today were likely the cashiers, food servers, and customer service representatives of yesterday. Typically, management will promote these individuals into their first supervisory position without providing appropriate basic training in management and the obligatory advanced training in customer service standards and expectations, although this is not always the case.

Consequently, these newly promoted supervisors are not fully conscious of what customer service is all about. They have not yet fully learned how important quality customer care is to a company's well-being, and they don't grasp the concept that they are responsible for ensuring that their employees provide superior customer care and services at all times. Indeed, that is the problem many new managers face, a lack of basic training. If you are in that boat, then you're off to a good start in getting the information you need with this book.

So, how should you manage an unhappy, vocal customer with a complaint? Here are six steps that will help you and your team:

- Be a great listener. Let the customer fully communicate his or her concerns, questions, and requests. Interrupt only to ask questions at appropriate times to show empathy and to fully understand the issue at hand. If the customer is upset and emotional, don't challenge his or her version of the facts or any of the customer's opinions. Let the customer vent. You want to avoid escalating the situation.

- Once the customer has fully conveyed the concerns. Acknowledge an understanding of the matter and apologize for any missteps the company may have made.

- Assess the magnitude of the problem at the time of the initial discussion with the customer. If the issue or request is minor and routine in nature, move forward to address the situation immediately. If the customer is very upset and emotional, or the nature of the problem requires research to identify the specifics surrounding the concern, then cordially end the discussion, indicating the need to research the circumstances surrounding the customer's concerns. Give the customer a specific time at which you or another appropriate team member will follow up with him or her.

- Thoroughly research the facts surrounding the customer's concerns. Things are not always as they appear.

- If your investigation determines that the customer's concerns are legitimate and that the problem requires a corrective action plan, implement the fix prior to following up with the customer, if possible. Then, by your commitment date, reach out to the customer and explain the results of your research and the corrective steps you have taken to ensure that the matter has been addressed.

- Thank your customer for bringing the concern to your attention. If appropriate, consider offering the customer some compensation suitable for the circumstances involved. Close by again apologizing for the inconveniences this customer has experienced.

- Ideally, you should require team members who encounter a customer complaint that is beyond their ability or authority to address to let you or another appropriate person know about the issue in a timely manner. This will ensure that the angry customer will receive a quick response instead of falling through the cracks.

Customer complaints are a fact of life in business. Your goal as a manager is to reduce the number of customer conflicts to as near zero as possible. Sometimes a problem stems from a poorly made product or a service that is not performed up to standards, but more often than not customers get angry because they have not been treated right. Treat your customers the way you would like to be treated, and like each one is your only customer.

Tips in a Nutshell

- The three types of customers—external, internal, and third party—all require superior customer service.
- Superior customer care is the lifeblood of any business.
- Customers should always be treated with respect.
- Include customer service performance on employee evaluations.
- Create a customer service minimum performance standards document and have all appropriate personnel sign it.
- Allow angry customers to vent, and then do whatever it reasonably takes to address the problem.
- Ultimately, it is your external customers who pay your company's expenses—including your paycheck. You therefore want to keep all of your customers happy all of the time.

9

Management in the Trenches

Companies are often compared to living creatures, or even people. I can see why. If you poke a business in one spot, you'll get a reflexive response that ripples through the entire organization. If the foot of a business is sore, then the whole company's ability to move through the daily challenges of operating at a profit will suffer. If a business receives a severe head injury because of stupid management decisions (it happens more often than you might think), then every single part of that business will either die a quick and traumatic death, or the company will linger in a coma until the creditors pull the plug.

I'm fine with comparing businesses to creatures. I also like comparing them to cars—call it a personal preference. But let's stick with the idea that a business lives, eats, and breathes, and that it is born, feels its growing pains through adolescence, matures into a vibrant and vital adult, and then progresses to a healthy or not-so-healthy old age. The business can get sick along the way, or a bus can run over it and squash out its life in a New York minute. Market collapses, supply chain demolitions, natural disasters, and many other negative external eventualities that management cannot control can threaten the existence of a company. But the most common cause of a sick or terminal business is bad management.

Over the years, I've been involved in turning around sick companies that somehow got off the track to success. It's often very challenging work. It's also always rewarding when the patient recovers and profitability returns. A balance sheet that once bled red ink that has now been changed to all black is like a cancer patient with a new lease on life. It's a reason to celebrate. As you make your way in a career in management, you'll start to see practices within the companies you work for that are akin to a person's bad habits, like smoking or drinking too much and so on. When you do, you have a choice to make. Do you do nothing and hope for the best? Do you shrug your shoulders and tell yourself it's not your job to fix something that's wrong in another department, even if it impacts directly on yours? Or do you take action to correct the problem?

Obviously, if you do nothing, the patient might get sick or sicker. If you take action to rid the patient of the bad habits and practices, then the prognosis for the future will be much brighter. When handled tactfully, presenting a well-conceived plan that offers solutions to the problem will help the company maintain or achieve good health, and it will also help you personally because your superiors will view you as a proactive manager. Such an individual will usually rise far in the corporate world, as long as he or she is also a skilled people person who pays attention to details large and small, in and out of assigned areas of responsibility.

Whether your managerial responsibilities are focused on sales, on operations, or on the financial side of the business, it is incumbent upon you as a management professional to actively work toward identifying and correcting deficiencies within your department, and in the organization as a whole, if it is possible and appropriate. Your responsibilities also include making vigilant efforts to reduce costs and exploit new business opportunities for the betterment of the company. Sometimes these opportunities are obvious and easy to capitalize on. In other cases, you need to take a step back, do some investigating, consult with employees, and think outside the box to identify and benefit from such opportunities. Rest assured that there is always room for improvement, even in a healthy patient or business.

Identifying deficiencies and new business opportunities will make you a proactive manager with a bright future.

When I am asked to manage an organization that is new to me, I employ a methodical approach right from the start to identify areas in need of improvement and avenues that might yield new opportunities to grow the business. Listening, gathering data, and clearly communicating are all part of the approach. I apply this approach even when I am working for apparently healthy companies, and I definitely use this method when I am told that the company is ill and in need of a helping hand from the top.

Step 1: I start out by asking staff and management many questions; where practical, I consult with virtually every person working within the organization. For larger businesses, I speak with a sampling of people from each department. I typically ask the same questions of everyone in my search for the facts.

Here are some of my favorite questions:

- If you owned the company, what would you do differently?
- What standard operating procedures are working and which ones are not?
- What can we do to make you more efficient at your job?
- Are you happy with your job? If not, why not?
- What can we do differently to ensure that our customers receive the best possible customer service and overall experience with the company?
- What can we do to make the company more efficient and profitable?
- What do you think are the biggest challenges for our company at this time? What major challenges are you dealing with in your department?

Step 2: While questioning team members, I do a thorough review of operations, and I begin to form my own opinions on what I think are possible solutions for a more desirable business management design.

Step 3: If I find myself working in a new industry or market area and coming up short with acceptable business solutions, I ask our team to shop our competitors and learn what they are doing right and where they are failing.

Step 4: Throughout the process, I interact and bounce various ideas (what ifs) off appropriate personnel in an effort to further refine and develop ideas for improving the existing business management design. I look for great ideas from our frontline people. I need them to be part of the fix-it process. I know staff and management may not agree with every new policy or procedure, but I not only want the feedback, I also want to increase the odds that everyone will take ownership and embrace the ultimate changes. Making employees and managers part of the process of both identifying areas where change is needed and also imparting the rationale behind those changes during the discovery process goes a long way toward easing concerns and lessening resistance. As I've said, bringing about change in a company is hard because people like to stay in their comfort zones—the status quo.

Stories from the Trenches

The following are a series of hypothetical business scenarios I dreamed up to demonstrate what I would do as a newly hired manager if I had to face a given challenge or problem. Although these fictitious stories are derived from my experience in businesses such as vending, you can easily apply the concepts to whatever industry you're in. As you immerse yourself in these stories, understand that the problems, analysis, and solutions in each one can serve as a roadmap in terms of critical thinking and problem solving. In essence, what I am trying to get you to do is think like a manager, which is much different from thinking like a staff member who has very limited job responsibilities. I explain the approach and strategies I would use to correct the business challenges at hand in each of the following stories.

Story 1

Troubled Wholesale Product Distributor

Background

The company in this story is a wholesaler of food-related products. Our company sells and distributes product to our customers via route salespeople. We also provide the equipment necessary for our customers to dispense these products to their customers (the end consumer). Our customers rely on us to keep our equipment in good working order and ensure that they do not run out of product, especially during their busy lunch and dinner hours.

We have several competitors in the marketplace who are forever approaching our customers and looking for our weaknesses (where we drop the customer-service ball in one way or another). In short, our competitors are looking to eat our lunch. Thus, it is important that we meet all the needs of our customers and that we do so in a timely manner.

I have just been hired to take over the management of this company.

The Challenge

At about nine o'clock in the morning, one hour into the first day of my new job, I was training with the departing manager, a guy named DJ. DJ took a phone call from one of our customers, a local social club calling to say they had run out of product. Without hesitation, DJ immediately stopped what he was doing, threw the required product in the back of his pickup truck, and said, "Come on, we have to go!" We were off. It was like we were firemen on our way to a fire. We could not get there fast enough. Then, to my surprise, I learned that the required product we had just rushed over with was for a special event scheduled for later in the evening. It was not exactly a drop-everything-emergency call.

DJ and I rushed out to several more "out of product" calls on that first day, and we did the same thing pretty much each day thereafter. Running out of product was not a good thing for our customers at any time, but it was especially problematic during their busy hours when our products were in most demand. While we only had about seventy accounts, we were averaging ten out-of-stock calls each day. Our office staff was fielding most of these calls, and they were spending a lot of time trying to appease our customers by promising almost immediate service. Typically, DJ, our service technician, and our route salesperson took care of the out-of-stock situations in a timely fashion (a short-term solution), but DJ took virtually no steps to minimize future out-of-stock calls (the long-term solution).

Can you imagine how inefficient this business was? Operating under those conditions was just plain silly—and totally unnecessary. Our customers were very upset at being out of product all the time and they continuously threatened to switch over to one of our competitors.

Analysis

As I went about my business observing and evaluating current practices, I began to suggest some "what ifs" to DJ, new ideas I thought would clearly help ease the customer service nightmare. I proposed encouraging some accounts to take on more inventory, and I suggested that perhaps it would be a good idea to educate other accounts on how their dispensing equipment worked, which in turn would empower them in an emergency. Regrettably, DJ said his business was built on good service and loyalty. To DJ, that meant when the customer asked him to jump, he'd ask how high.

When a customer called DJ, he did not walk, he ran. He ran morning, noon, and night to fulfill each customer's request. DJ was convinced that if he did not rush to meet the requests, someone else would. That point of view and practice helped explain why he was burnt out and looking to leave the company. DJ did not believe you could or should ask customers to help you help them succeed in their businesses. He did not believe that he should educate them regarding the benefits of taking on some extra inventory and perhaps some minor equipment responsibilities that would help us keep their product costs down and reduce equipment downtime (a true business partnership).

Upon further analysis and investigation, it turned out there were a myriad of reasons for the recurring out-of-stock calls. Some accounts were not on a preplanned delivery schedule. They were asked to call our office for product deliveries when they were low or had actually run out. That was usually done because of perceived product room constraints. In other cases, accounts had plenty of room for product but also carried low levels of inventory, which was not always enough to carry them over until their next scheduled delivery day. For example, a customer could have sufficient product on hand to meet their needs one week, but then run out of product two weeks in a row.

The chaos and frequent need to pull our delivery person off his scheduled route to address out-of-stock calls created more trouble. He was unable to complete his assigned route on most days, which caused additional out-of-stock conditions. Unfortunately, there were times when our very own warehouse would run out of certain products, and we were unable to meet the needs of our customers even when we did show up on their scheduled delivery days. Finally, our dispensing equipment in the field experienced many issues, sometimes even becoming inoperative.

Our customers relied on us to professionally and accurately assess and meet their product needs on a consistent basis. If we did not get it right, the customers would look elsewhere for a supplier who could better meet their needs. From a customer-service perspective, it was absolutely imperative that we respond to out-of-product calls in a timely manner (the short-term solution). However, it was equally important to identify why an account ran out of product (even if it was just once in a six-month period), and then implement an appropriate action plan to help minimize the chance of a future out-of-stock condition (the long-term solution).

The Fix

After identifying the various causes of our perpetual out-of-stock conditions and other operational challenges, I wrote up an action plan outlining new initiatives, specific goals, and procedures to address virtually all of our service-delivery issues. I then sat down with my team members to discuss the plan and to tweak it as needed based on their feedback.

The fix consisted of the following:

- Going forward, rather than calling our office when running low on a particular product, every customer would be put on a specific schedule for delivery.

- We reviewed each account's weekly sales volume, current inventory on hand, and the available space allocated for our product. With this information, we adjusted customer inventory levels, usually increasing the quantities and hooked up product containers in tandem via product lines. This allowed us to service accounts less frequently without customers running out of product. We left extra product at account locations when we were made aware of upcoming customer special events or other activities that might affect an account's historical usage. We then taught our customers how to change product containers in the event of an emergency situation.

- We trained our route salesperson to track account product usage between deliveries and to make inventory adjustments accordingly. This usually resulted in increasing inventory levels to help prevent out-of-stock conditions as a customer's business grew.

- We equipped our route salesperson with some simple tools and a small inventory of the equipment parts that were most likely to fail in the field. He was empowered to make minor repairs as he encountered equipment problems while servicing our accounts. When a problem was beyond the capabilities of our route salesperson to fix, he was directed to call in a service-repair request (for our technician to address) prior to moving on to his next stop. It was a priority to repair all equipment problems in a timely manner.

- With this new delivery plan in place, our route salesperson was able (and expected) to finish his route as scheduled each day.

- We informed our customers of what we were doing. We educated them on how their product systems worked. We asked that they work with us so that we could provide them with superior customer service and effectively manage down their overall product costs.

Most customers were very appreciative and supportive of our efforts. There were a few who complained about having to purchase extra inventory to help accommodate our new business management design, but we were able to address their concerns with some free product. At the end of the day, our new design proved to be a winner for all parties. Out-of-stock calls dropped to virtually zero, and customers no longer stressed over having no product on hand during peak business hours. Everyone's sales volume rose significantly. We were now maximizing sales and creating a highly positive experience for our customers.

Lessons Learned

It became very clear to me that the company needed a complete overhaul in terms of how it was run. As it turned out, it did. Prompt and decisive action in the face of a challenge created a healthier business for us—and especially for each of our customers.

- Manage your company proactively utilizing sound business principles.
- Always look for the short- and long-term solutions to your business problems.
- Do not let your business manage you.

Story 2

A Company without Unity

Background

The company in this story is a wholesaler comprised of three departments. The firm sells many different food products. Each department sells in its own market channels.

I am the newly hired manager for the smallest of these three departments, Department B. I am the most junior member of the management team.

The Challenge

The company was not performing as expected overall. As noted above, the company consisted of three distinct business units operating under one roof. Department A sold products through supermarkets and convenience stores (known as the take-home market). Department B (my new department) distributed products via restaurants and bars (the on-premises market). Department C also sold products through restaurants, bars, and retail stores.

The company would have greatly benefited as a whole had all three departments actively supported each other internally and in the marketplace, participating in cross-marketing promotions and so on. However, for a variety of reasons, the company operated more like three independently owned businesses than like a cohesive team. The culture was not one of great cooperation and unity, to say the least. Almost as soon as I began working there, I realized it was pretty much every manager for himself or herself.

Analysis

From my viewpoint, the primary challenge I was facing in my quest for growing my business was the lack of cooperation and support from the other departments. I was the junior manager in the company, and I had virtually no authority or power outside my department.

I was not under the impression that I couldn't grow my business without internal support and help from the company's senior managers, but I did conclude that all three business units (the company as a whole) could have greatly benefited in the short- and the long-term with a little support and cooperation among the three departments.

The Fix

When I took over the business, the market share for my department was so small and the sales volume was so low that I knew my sales numbers would increase dramatically if I picked up just a handful of new accounts. I had nowhere to go but up.

The fix consisted of the following:

- My first task was to learn more about the marketplace and our competitors. I needed to gain knowledge of their reputations in the market, strengths (best practices) and weaknesses, equipment and product offerings, pricing and promotional activity, and so on.

- I then set out to visit bars, restaurants, colleges, and other venues throughout my market area to introduce myself to managers and owners. I asked if they were happy with their current supplier. The results were mixed, though in most cases I was given the opportunity to assess their dispensing equipment. I often identified deficiencies and pinpointed the range of problems the business was having with the equipment. At that point, I gained instant credibility, and owners and managers were interested in listening to my pitch.

  The more restaurant surveys I did, the more vulnerable my competitors appeared to be. Their equipment appeared old, inefficient, and not well maintained. Some customers complained about poor service and frequently being out of stock. I was also able to offer other business solutions, products, and services that my competitors were unable or unwilling to provide. I began to promote the one-stop-shopping concept. Our company was able to meet all the product needs of our customers.

- My department's stock began to go up in the eyes of our other sales departments as I began to have some success selling many of our products into key account restaurants. Many of these accounts had been carrying only a minimum amount of the products sold by our other departments. After building a good rapport with the restaurant owners, I began to encourage them to carry all of our product lines. I then introduced them to the salespeople from our other departments.

- Eventually, Department C salespeople began to introduce me to the restaurant owners they had loyal relationships with. New business continued to breed new business, and I continued to promote the one-stop-shopping concept.

- I began to convert fast food restaurants, colleges, and other such accounts to our brands. Those accounts brought new sales opportunities to Department A's sales team. Those salespeople began cooperating with my department. They referred me to the key account managers whom they had awesome relationships with.

- We began to run market-wide promotions as one company, tying the three business units together. That way we all could take advantage of the marketing and promotional dollars offered up by our national brand suppliers.

At the end of the day, our management team, sales staff, and support personnel came to understand the value of a unified workforce pulling together for the benefit of the company as a whole.

Lessons Learned

- The benefits and synergies obtained through teamwork and a unified effort should not be ignored.

Story 3

Demand Run Wild

Background

The company in this story is a manufacturer and wholesaler of many different food products. Our company's main facility houses our production operations, which provide product for our local market and for a dozen other distribution points within our state. Our company's sales volume has grown exponentially over the past ten years because of several business acquisitions. Although our production facility has the capacity to meet the growing demand, the dramatic increase in production and the ultimate distribution of the products created other operating challenges at the facility.

I have just been hired to manage the business.

The Challenge

While production at our plant had increased substantially over the years, the business management design was the same one put in place fifteen years earlier when the plant began operations. Sales volume was obviously much lower at that time.

We were using a concept called "just in time delivery," which was (and is) fairly common in high-volume production facilities. For example, when all of our production lines were running at full capacity, it could require up to ten tractor-trailer trucks full of various raw goods to feed them each and every hour. It would be logistically impossible to warehouse the required supplies prior to an eight- or ten-hour production run. Instead, we scheduled trucks to arrive at our loading docks exactly when we needed the goods to keep operations going.

On any given day, a portion of the day's production was held back and diverted to a section of the warehouse used to load our local market delivery trucks. The loading process for those route trucks, and the traffic flow in and around the plant were the areas of most concern. Solutions were needed to improve operations.

The challenges included the following:

- There was very little exterior space available for staging and parking the incoming and outgoing trucks that serviced the production lines. That could be somewhat problematic since there could be as many as eighty tractor-trailers coming and going on a full production day. Adding to that traffic dilemma were the thirty local delivery trucks serving our local market.

- Local delivery trucks needed to load each night. The process was currently a disaster in terms of safety and productivity. The loading crew routinely worked through the night, sometimes fourteen hours at a time (working many hours of overtime with much fatigue). In spite of those heroic efforts, route trucks were very often loaded incorrectly and were not always ready in time for our route drivers, whose workdays sometimes began at 6:00 a.m.

- Safety was also a very big concern because bottle breakage was a common occurrence during the loading process. The breakage left liquid product strewn around the warehouse floor virtually every night, making for very hazardous working conditions. Forklifts loaded with pallets of product had a very difficult time maneuvering and stopping on the wet, sticky floors.

- Because of the massive mess left by the truck-loading team each morning, the day crew in the warehouse rarely had time to adequately clean up and restock the loading area prior to the loading crew resuming its late-afternoon shifts. We had a perpetual cycle of operational dysfunction in the truck-loading area of the warehouse.

- Morale was very low. Truck loaders and route sales staff blamed each other for the ongoing problems.

Analysis

I spent my first few days on the project observing the traffic flow of all exterior truck activity. I focused on the incoming and outgoing tractor-trailers supporting the production lines and on how those vehicles interacted with our company's local delivery trucks throughout the day. A few days later, I spent several nights working with the truck-loading crew. I interviewed all eight loaders individually and asked each of them the same questions to get a better sense of what they thought was and was not working. I asked what they would do differently if they owned the company. The interviews confirmed my own observations.

I next met separately with the truck-loading supervisor and with the route managers. I asked them what they thought was and was not working. I asked what they would do differently if they could. I then asked each of the managers to tell me what was really important to them with regard to the truck-loading operation.

Not surprisingly, they all had different points of view. The night supervisor was actually on track with some of his thoughts and ideas, but the route-management team wouldn't agree to implement his proposals. The night supervisor lacked the authority to unilaterally implement the changes he wanted to make. Unfortunately, the route managers were only looking out for what was best for them and their sales team, not what was in the best interest of the company as a whole. If all parties had communicated and worked together to effect changes that would help everyone, all or most of the problems could have been avoided. Such thinking often falls on the shoulders of a general manager for that very reason. Department heads sometimes will not cooperate.

I observed and noted in writing several areas of concern during my evaluation:

- The sales department's loading policies appeared to be designed to appease route personnel. What might be in the best interest of the company did not seem to matter.

- There was little, if any, effective communication between route managers and the truck-loading supervisor.

- There was no established traffic flow for end-of-day returning local market route trucks.

- Poorly designed check-in procedures did not adequately prepare route trucks for night loading.

- The quantity and percentage of unsold product (by brand, package, and size) coming back on route trucks at the end of each day was not noted, which made it impossible to adjust loads to better suit actual demand.

- No established, standardized truck-loading procedures or guidelines existed.

- There were no standard operating procedures for tracking truck-loading errors and productivity. No process existed for improving either area.

- The warehouse was not laid out strategically (e.g., placing product by flavor, package type, and size in the loading area to maximize efficiencies).

The Fix

The observations I made during the discovery phase of my new management position were disturbing, but they weren't surprising. When management fails to give a business a thorough physical exam on a regular basis, one problem will create another and so on down the road. In this case, the neglect had been severe. The patient was very sick. Fortunately, the treatment was fairly straightforward. The fix consisted of the following:

- The rear side of the facility was virtually unused. It offered a fair amount of room and a simple solution for reducing the traffic congestion in front of the plant, which was heavily used by commercial vehicles servicing the production lines. We rerouted local route trucks upon their return to the plant. Route salespeople were now required to utilize the rear entrance driveway of the warehouse whenever they returned to the plant. If their routes were completed for the day, route sales staff was required to proceed to a specific area of the warehouse to check in. The staff members parked their trucks in assigned areas where truck loaders could easily access them later in the evening.

- During the check-in process, route salespeople were now required to remove all empty containers and product breakage from their trucks. They were also required to reorganize the product on their trucks, if necessary. Those extra efforts prepared the trucks for loading, which increased the productivity of the truck loaders.

- We established a new system-wide goal for route sales-people to manage end-of-day truck inventories to 30 percent or less of the original load. Route supervisors were required to monitor the amount of product coming back on their respective route trucks. The route supervisors coached and retrained the route salespeople to ensure they were managing truck inventories as per the new policies.

Prior to the implementation of the new policy, many trucks were returning at the end of each day with as much as 70 percent of the original load of product. That was unreasonable, as it unnecessarily increased truck-loading times, added needless wear and tear to the trucks, and reduced the fuel mileage of the overloaded vehicles. The excess inventory on route trucks also contributed to product having extremely short in-store shelf life because much of the product rode around on trucks for weeks at a time before it was sold.

- We implemented new product-loading guidelines for route sales staff. These included a truck loading plan-o-gram that standardized where specific products were to be loaded. For example, we stipulated that cans and bagged items were to be loaded on the driver's side of the truck, and that bottles and boxed items were to be loaded on the passenger side of the truck. The concept allowed us to preload and stage the warehouse similarly with cans and bagged items placed on the driver's side of the warehouse, and bottles and boxed items on the passenger side of the truck loading area.

- We required truck loaders to begin working in teams of two when loading trucks for a given shift. One loader was responsible for loading the driver's side of the truck, and the other was responsible for loading the passenger side. They were now required to sign their names on load sheets for each truck they loaded and indicate their load start and finish times. That helped to promote productivity and hold night loaders accountable for load errors. It also helped get the competitive juices flowing among the night loaders, which also contributed to increased productivity.

- We established routine cooperative communications between route sales staff, truck loaders, and the appropriate members of the management team. At that point, everyone recognized the value of cooperation and finding solutions that were best for the company as a whole.

All these initiatives collectively resolved the traffic flow issues in and around our facility, greatly improved morale, and increased loading efficiencies.

Lessons Learned

Junior managers who make self-serving decisions that are not in the best interest of the company are very common. Obviously, managers need to make decisions that best serve the entire company, not just what's best for their respective departments or what fulfills their own self-serving interests.

For example, the following scenario would not be financially healthy or in the best interests of the company (all things being equal). Say a junior manager implemented a new policy that saved his or her department five grand in annual expenses. Sounds like a winner? But consider that the policy actually cost the entire company ten grand in annual expenses. Sounds like a loser, right? Right! Managers need to consider and factor in the potential negative impact their decisions may have on other departments prior to implementing any new policies. Do not allow this kind of self-serving behavior to occur in your team on your watch. When you keep your finger on the pulse of your business and stay engaged with your team, you, your department, and the company will all win.

In my world and in an effort to help our team make decisions that are in the best interest of the company, I request that all department heads and their appropriate support staff meet at least once every other week as a team. We call these gatherings operation's meetings, and they're all about communicating with each other. The group discusses current and upcoming projects, existing and proposed procedure and policy initiatives, and anything else that may involve or affect multiple departments.

As a team, they identify what is working and what is not among their departments. They look for opportunities to increase sales, reduce expenses, and improve both intra- and inter-departmental efficiencies. Above all else, the team constantly looks for ways to make the customer's experience with us more positive and rewarding than ever. Minutes are written up and distributed to all in attendance.

- Consider what impact your business decisions will have on other people in and out of your department.
- Always work in the best interests of the company and don't put your own department ahead of others out of self-interest.
- Resist unilaterally implementing new polices and procedures.

Story 4

Overcoming Competitive and Market Challenges

Background

An investor group has just purchased a full-line vending company in need of a helping hand. The company sells an assortment of products via various types of vending machines. Some of the products include soda, juice, candy, snacks, coffee, and fresh food.

I've been brought aboard to manage the vending company, but I'm new to the industry and need to learn it. I also need to learn how our company currently functions.

The Challenge

The vending company had been very successful when the investor group purchased it. However, there were two new market challenges beginning to emerge that the investor group didn't know about prior to the acquisition. These challenges became painfully obvious as soon as I took over.

- One of our company's primary product lines was losing favor with our customers, who were becoming interested in another brand name we didn't carry. Unfortunately, the product line that was losing ground to the competing brand represented 20 percent of the company's revenue at the time of the acquisition. Sales were falling fast. With revenue dramatically going down and operating expenses climbing steadily, our bottom line was heading south.

- The second challenge centered on a new wave of unscrupulous start-up vending companies entering our market. Vending operators typically look for locations they believe to be viable for their machines, and then they negotiate with the potential clients, offering to pay for the privilege of placing machines at their location. When the prospecting company discovers that another vending company is already doing business at a location, the prospecting company will sometimes offer to pay a higher commission (a percentage of machine sales) to the potential client.

In general, private businesses want to keep vending prices low as a benefit for employees, but they may also seek a small commission income. In government offices and public locations like airports, hotels, and resorts, vending prices are normally higher than average, and so are commission rates. Under normal bidding circumstances, the highest commission rate typically wins the contract (25 percent versus 20 percent of the gross sales of a specific vending machine, for example).

Soon after the investor group hired me, I discovered that some of the new competing vending operators were not always honest and would bid very unrealistic (high) commission rates. The commitments were sometimes too high for a company to sustain a healthy profit margin. To compensate for this, these operators would then manipulate the actual sales figures down in their sales reports to clients to effectively understate account revenue. By doing so, the vending companies competing with us were actually paying fewer commission dollars to their clients than were actually earned under the terms of the agreement. Of course, that kind of activity made it very difficult for an honest operator to compete.

Analysis

Our overall mission was to find a way to quickly offset the effects of the lost revenue. We needed to maximize vendor sales, retain our existing account base, acquire new business, and reduce our operating expenses while controlling our cost of goods. The bottom line was we had to aggressively and methodically increase sales revenue, reduce expenses, and effectively beat back the new competitors.

In an effort to better learn the industry and how our vending company functioned, I spent my first two weeks on the job working alongside a different route salesperson each day. I loaded trucks, filled out paperwork, filled and cashed out vending machines, and met with our account contacts. In the third week, I worked in the warehouse shadowing our warehouse crew. I then worked with each of our route sales supervisors, asking lots of questions, and then I consulted with our senior managers to discuss my findings. My observations included the following:

- We were carrying an excessive selection of products in our warehouse.

- There was no rationale for what route salespeople placed into their respective vending machines. There was no established plan-o-gram to direct what kinds of product should be placed in a given vending machine or where they should be placed.

- Most accounts seemed to be over serviced. Vending machines were often 70 percent full at the time of service. Yet, machines would regularly run out of the top-selling items between service calls, creating an out-of-stock condition. Unfortunately, that meant customers were unable to purchase the products they were looking for, which resulted in lost sales revenue and lost confidence in us.

- Our account contacts were not thrilled with the product selections being offered in their soda, snack, and food vending machines. They had infrequent contact with our route personnel, and they were rarely consulted on what they would like to see placed in their machines.

- Machines were unnecessarily being "cashed out" on virtually every service call, meaning that all the money was removed when the machine was being filled. While it was costly to carry out a simple "fill" service to a machine (to fill it with product only, with no cash collected), it was more expensive to perform a "full-service" call, which included filling and cashing out the machine. For example, when cash was collected, the product in the machine had to be counted prior to filling it for cash-reconciliation purposes. Kind of like reconciling your checkbook at home. The full-service calls added considerable service time to a route, which resulted in fewer vending machines being serviced in a given day. That brought route efficiencies down.

Additionally, every collected cash bag had to be counted and processed back at the office. The more bags there were, the more time was needed to get the job done. It was more efficient to process and count a bag with three hundred dollars in it than it was to count a bag three different times with one hundred dollars in each tally. There was also more opportunity for errors with each cash-collecting transaction, which then required additional personnel time to find and correct the error.

- The amount of spoilage being returned by route sales staff was high and above industry averages.

- Our route sales personnel were paid a fixed weekly salary regardless of how many hours they worked or how much sales revenue they generated on their respective routes. There was no incentive in place for route salespeople to care or be concerned about what products were placed in the machines.

The Fix

After much discussion with our management team, we developed a new business management design that included the following actions:

- We scaled back on the number of product types in our warehouse. The reduced stockroom selections supported our new vendor plan-o-grams, which collectively helped to reduce company-wide inventory levels. It also lowered spoilage rates. The change helped to increase our warehouse inventory turns.

- We identified and ranked the top-selling soda, snack, and fresh food products for our company, and we created plan-o-grams for each type and size vendor. We customized these plans to meet the needs of each of our accounts. We incorporated a concept I called space-to-sales, where we allocated more space in the machines to the items that sold well and less to those that did not. Yet, we still used the full capacity of the vending machine (when and where practical). More specifically, we wanted to stock each machine with enough of each product so as not to run out of any one item between service calls, regardless of the sales volume.

- We adjusted the "fill" only and the "fill-and-collect" service frequencies of each vendor so machines would be approximately 70 percent empty at the time of service. We wanted to take full advantage of the vending machine's product capacity. There was no sense in placing a soda or snack machine at a location that held five hundred cans of soda or snack items and then servicing it when the machine was still 70 percent full. That would be like going to the gas station every other day to top off your vehicle's sixteen-gallon fuel tank with two or three gallons of gas. Cash was also collected from vending machines less frequently, usually at every other or every third fill, subject to the machine's volume. Route salespeople were able to service twice the number of vending machines each week with the new business management design.

- In an effort to build rapport and learn what was important to our accounts, route salespeople were required to connect with appropriate account contacts on a routine basis.

- When route sales personnel earned a weekly fixed salary, they functioned more like truck drivers than salespeople. They were not motivated to maximize the sales potential of each vending machine on their routes. To help remedy that, we restructured our routes and altered how we paid route personnel going forward. Route sales staff under the new business management design would be paid on a commission basis—a percentage of their respective route sales revenue for each week they worked. They no longer earned a weekly salary. They now had a vested interest in learning what soda and snack items our customers wanted in the machines, and they were motivated to recognize and learn which items sold and which did not in each of their assigned vending machines.

Among other things, the changes allowed us to eliminate many vending routes. This resulted in substantial savings in both fleet and labor costs. Remaining route sales personnel earned much more money with this new business management design. We wanted all route salespeople to be creative and connected to each account in an effort to maximize customer satisfaction and to maximize sales at every vending machine. It worked. Our accounts were happy, and we held the unscrupulous competitors at bay, driving them from our market areas.

Lessons Learned

- Responding quickly to competitive and operational challenges stopped the downward spiral of the company.
- Refining product selection to match customer demand improved customer service and sales.
- If you are new to an industry, take the time to learn about it and the current business management design of your company as you move toward making improvements and addressing business challenges.

10

Taking Your Company's Financial Pulse

Business is all about profitability. If a business fails to generate profits after expenses, you can bet that company won't last very long in today's competitive marketplace. It's not enough to have high gross revenues if expenses eliminate the margin of profitability. High sales volumes don't necessarily translate into heaps of money at the end of the day, even though it might seem like a business is thriving because everyone is so busy and money appears to be flowing in.

To put it another way, if you spend ten bucks to get a nine-dollar return on your investment, you've lost a dollar. The business failed to make a profit—and even worse, it lost money. In addition to ensuring profitability, a company must increase its gross profit dollars sufficiently enough each year to stay ahead of inflation. This can be accomplished by increasing product sales volume, and by increasing gross profit margins via higher retail prices or lower product costs. While it is unlikely that as a new manager you will be responsible for decisions that make or break profitability for the entire company, it is a very good idea to be mindful of the major concept as you go about fulfilling your duties. Someday, you may very well find yourself at the helm, and you'll need to know what to do. At the very least, you are already in charge of a department or business unit, and the financial side of running that part of the business is already your responsibility.

To help ensure the financial health of a business, the accounting department produces various types of financial statements on a regular basis to track the company's performance for a given time period. Each of these reports presents different pieces of information in various formats. Think of financial statements as report cards. They help you see how well you did in the previous month compared to budget and how you are doing this year compared to last year during the same period. Running and tracking the numbers is vital because doing so can help you identify trends that impact negatively or positively on the bottom line. Business owners, corporate accountants, controllers, and chief financial officers will be interested in reading the many different financial reports, such as balance sheets, owner equity statements, corporate retained earnings, and cash flow reports. Frontline and midlevel managers typically need only be familiar with profit and loss statements (and product inventory reports if you are managing a business or department that has inventory).

When you examine the numbers, you will no doubt find an interesting story, and that story will change based on market conditions, rising or falling demand, and many additional factors. The numbers can tell us that we exceeded the budget for costs of goods or operating expenses in a given month, and we will want to find out why. The numbers can tell if we fell behind projected profits for that same period. Again, we will want to know why. What is driving the numbers? Has a decrease in profit stemmed from an unexpectedly high cost for the goods we sold? Has it resulted from lowering the price for the goods during a special promotional campaign? The reasons for fluctuations in the numbers are too numerous to list here, but let's just say that you can't formulate an action plan to address a negative trend in profitability if you don't know there's a problem in the first place.

Your daily responsibilities as a manager go beyond simply managing through the day's operational and business challenges. You need to make a profit and control expenses. You need to understand the details of your budget and your profit and loss statements, as well as what makes up the numbers you are looking at. For example, you may have observed a positive trend on your income statement, such as lower-than-expected operating costs. After taking the time to investigate why, you learn one of your employees took the initiative to tweak the daily work routine, which saved the company a substantial amount of money. Your efforts to learn why these costs were below those projected in the overall plan now give you the opportunity to recognize the rock star employee on your team. Sharing what the employee did that saved money with other employees will further reduce costs if everybody else follows suit, and it will help create a corporate culture where innovative ideas to cut expenses are encouraged and rewarded.

Profit and loss statements are like a report card on a company's performance for a given period of time.

In the following pages, I will explain how to read and analyze a profit and loss statement. We're going to take a close look at how ABC Hat Company performed in May, and we'll see that the numbers indeed tell us a story. First, let's look at the following financial terms as a way to get started. Be aware that people often use these terms somewhat loosely. Some category line items you'll find on a profit and loss statement have multiple names. For example, gross sales, sales, gross revenue, revenue, and "the top line" all can refer to the same line item. Gross profit is sometimes called net revenue, and net operating income is often referred to as net operating profit. The terminology will vary from industry to industry, by geographic regions, and even from person to person within a company.

Budget

When you think of a budget, it's natural to compare it to a family budget for housing, food, transportation, and other expenses associated with maintaining a household. At home, the budget represents the expense side of the ledger, and your net pay represents the profit side. Companies run budgets like that too, but we also project (or budget) for income. When assessing the performance of a company in a given time period, it's important to calculate how much gross revenue is expected to come in and how much cash is expected to go out to cover expenses.

Profit and loss statement

A profit and loss statement (P&L) simply shows a company's revenue, expenses, and net profit or loss. The cost of the goods it provides for customers is deducted from the gross sales, as are operating expenses. The end result is the company's net operating income for a specific time period. The report usually presents actual performance numbers in a comparative line with the current year's budget and the previous year's numbers. A P&L statement is also known as an income or a financial statement.

Gross Sales

Gross sales, or revenue, reflect the total dollars the company took in during the financial period.

Cost of goods (COGS)

Cost of goods is what you pay to acquire or make the product you intend to sell. For example, if it cost you three dollars to make a hat, that's your cost of goods. You also have to factor in the hats that did not sell because of a defect or loss (inventory shrinkage). You still had to pay for the damaged or lost hats you didn't sell, so those costs count when calculating cost of goods.

Gross profit

Gross profit equals the net of gross sales less the cost of goods. These are very important dollars. They are used to pay all operating expenses associated with the business, including your salary. As you pursue your new duties, always remember that a golden rule to live by in any business is to do whatever is reasonable to preserve as much of the gross profit as you can without sacrificing customer service, product quality, or operating efficiencies.

Operating expenses

Operating expenses can cover just about anything related to running the business—building rent, staffing, office supplies, and repairs/ maintenance (R&M) for such items as vehicles, equipment, the building you operate out of, and so on. General operating expenses are not included in cost of goods.

Net operating income

At home this would be what's left in your checking account when you're finished paying off all your bills at the end of the month. In business and on your P&L report, this is the net of gross sales minus cost of goods and operating expenses. Companies can't function for long in a red-ink world. They go bankrupt. Companies must maintain a positive net operating profit over the long term if they are to survive and thrive.

Inventory shrinkage

The loss of inventory through a non-sales event is called inventory shrinkage, and it has to be factored into your cost of goods analysis. Destroyed, damaged, spoiled, or defective products, along with customer and employee theft of products, represent the most common types of inventory shrinkage. Controlling inventory shrinkage should be a primary concern of the entire management team and all its subordinates. While some industries face more inventory challenges than others, the bottom line is that every company has its own set of unique product and inventory control burdens. If inventory control is part of your responsibility, you must rise to the challenge and effectively manage it if you are to maximize profitability.

Here's a look at ABC Hat Company's May P&L statement for illustration purposes.

Although most companies customize P&L statements to reflect what is most important to management and the firm's business model, the headings, revenue, and expense line items incorporated in the sample statement below are good representations of what you're likely to see in your new job. The company's name, the report name (type of information being reported), and the date range of reported business activity go up on top. In the example below, the date for the five months ending May 31, 2011, indicates that this income statement presents the financial activity of ABC Hat Company for the month of May and, collectively, the financial information for the first five months of the fiscal year (January through May 2011).

The column headings in our sample for May's statement are as follows:

- "Actual" reflects the actual financial activity for the month.
- "Budget" reflects the budget numbers for the month.
- "Previous Year Actual" reflects actual financial activity for the month of May in 2010 (the previous fiscal year). One of the beauties of a P&L statement is that it provides an easy way to compare present company performance to the previous year's performance.
- "YTD Actual" reflects actual financial activity for the first five months of the current fiscal year (2011). YTD stands for year-to-date.
- "YTD Budget" reflects the budget numbers for the first five months of the current fiscal year (2011).
- "Previous YTD Actual" reflects actual financial activity for the first five months of 2010 (the previous fiscal year).

Sales revenue and expense line items listed along the left side of the report begin with revenue at the top followed by product cost of goods, gross profit, and then the operating costs directly associated with ABC Hat Company. The net operating income line follows expenses for operations, sales, administration, and payroll. The line reflects the net of total revenue minus the cost of goods and all operating costs. Reducing the net operating income by the last two non-operating expense line items (depreciation and interest expenses) gives the company's net income figure.

ABC Hat Company

Profit & Loss Statement

For the Five Months Ending May 31, 2011

	May Actual	May Budget	May Prev. Year Actual	May YTD Actual	May YTD Budget	May Prev. YTD Actual
Gross Sales	$25,000	19,000	16,000	125,000	110,000	95,000
COGS	7,500	6,500	6,200	47,500	32,500	31,000
Gross Profit	17,500	12,500	9,800	77,500	77,500	64,000
Building Rent	700	600	500	3,500	3,000	2,500
Building R&M	100	100	100	400	400	1,900
Equipment R&M	100	100	100	1,000	600	600
Vehicle R&M	100	100	100	100	500	500
Vehicle Fuel	100	100	100	500	500	500
Utilities	200	200	200	1,500	1,500	2,000
Total Opt. Exp.	1,300	1,200	1,100	7,000	6,500	8,000
Advertising	400	300	400	1,500	1,500	1,500
Business, Meals	100	150	100	600	750	500
Postage/ Shipping	100	200	250	1,000	1,000	1,200
Telephone	200	150	200	800	750	800

Office Expenses	300	250	200	900	1,000	900
Total Sales Exp.	1,100	1,050	1,150	4,800	5,000	4,900
Legal Exp.	400	300	300	900	1,500	1,300
Accounting	200	100	200	500	500	500
Insurance	400	300	250	1,500	1,500	1,300
Total Admin.	1,000	700	750	2,900	3,500	3,100
Payroll	4,000	4,000	3,500	20,000	20,000	17,000
Total Payroll	4,000	4,000	3,500	20,000	20,000	17,000
Net Opt. Inc.	10,100	5,550	3,300	42,800	42,500	31,000
Depreciation	3,000	3,000	3,000	15,000	15,000	15,000
Interest Exp.	1,000	1,000	1,000	5,000	5,000	5,000
Total Misc. Exp	4,000	4,000	4,000	20,000	20,000	20,000
Net Income	6,100	1,550	(700)	22,800	22,500	11,000

After carefully reading ABC Hat Company's P&L statement, what conclusions have you drawn?

The above P&L statement is very revealing in several different ways. Before I share my own observations with you, why not take a few more minutes to look at the statement one more time. Remember, this is an exercise designed to help you see how an experienced manager would look at the data. Don't worry if you miss something. You probably will. You'll master the P&L statement soon enough.

The first thing I look at when I receive the monthly P&L statement is the current month's revenue versus the budget, and then I look at the YTD revenue versus YTD budget. I then glance down to the net operating income to compare it with the budget. Next, I review each expense line item, both current and YTD, and compare it to the budget. I highlight each line item where there appears to be a significant variance in comparison to the budget. I also look for trends (good and not so good), and if I see any anomalies in the current month's numbers, I start investigating to learn why. If need be, I'll involve other appropriate personnel in my efforts to fully understand and verify the figures that appear to be out of budget range.

As I've said before, communication is a vital part of your job as a manager. If you see something on a P&L statement that requires further explanation, it's your responsibility to find the answers. Once you have learned the reasons for the numbers, you can decide whether you need to implement an action plan to correct the deficiency. If there is good news, like an unexpected upward trend in net operating income, you need to find out what caused that positive outcome for the month and if appropriate share best practices with others. Best practices are refined procedures that result in better outcomes than what current practices provide. Simply put, a best practice is a better way of doing something.

After examining all operating expenses, I take a close look at product costs and the gross profit line. As part of my product cost-of-goods analysis, I also review product inventory levels and inventory turnover from other financial and product inventory reports.

Rest assured, you will inevitably encounter a P&L statement where revenue and expenses will occasionally come in significantly above or below budget for the month, yet YTD totals will still be in line with the plan. In other cases, there will be an obvious explanation for the discrepancy, and no further investigation or action will be required.

Company performance numbers can vary from budget from time to time with good reason.

In business, few things are mysterious, at least not for the long term. Some variations in a P&L statement can be easily explained. Here are a couple of examples:

- Sometimes annual budget numbers are allocated for the year in a straight-lined format. If the budget is set up in this way, an annual estimate for revenue of $120,000 divided by twelve months would show up as projected monthly revenue of $10,000. Sounds simple, right?

But it's not so simple in real life. A company's actual sales volume can be seasonal. In other words, it may fluctuate based on demand. If you straight-lined the estimate for monthly revenue, your P&L statement in the slow months would show a downward trend in actual revenue as compared to what was expected. Nobody should be overly alarmed, however. Typically, in a case like this, notes would have been attached to the budget to explain such expected discrepancies. And of course your year-to-date sales numbers should come in line with expected figures over time as you enter the busy season.

These seasonal variations are compelling reasons for companies to adjust and weight their expected sales and expenses during the budget-building process in an effort to align budget numbers with expected month-to-month activity. Of course, straight lining is better if expected variations are relatively minor.

- Many companies now pay employees on a bi-weekly basis, usually resulting in two pay periods per fiscal period (typically one calendar month). However, there may be times throughout the year when payroll expenses will hit the financials three times in a single month. Naturally, this will negatively impact your P&L statement in those months if the budget did not factor in those additional costs. However, in this scenario, all things being equal, the actual versus the budget YTD numbers should balance themselves out over the subsequent months. Again, such a variation should be no cause for alarm.

My observations regarding ABC Hat Company's performance will include a review of both its P&L statement and its product inventory levels.

You can obtain additional important information about your company's financial performance and identify possible business-improving opportunities by tracking your product inventory levels (total product on hand) in terms of units and dollars. Monitoring actual product costs and resale price points per unit sold as compared to your budget values is often very important.

For example, let's assume the following resale price points, product unit costs, and percentages (ratios) were used to build the budget in the above P&L statement for ABC Hat Company. If each hat sells for ten dollars and it costs three dollars to make a hat, then the gross sales profit on each hat is seven dollars. Let's further assume that ABC's end-of-month inventory value for the past year has averaged $20,000 and that the company orders and receives shipments of hats every week. In this example, I have not accounted for variations due to lost or destroyed hats (inventory shrinkage). So, take a look at what the numbers tell you so far:

Cost of goods = 30 percent of sales ($3 / $10 = 30%)
Product markup = 233 percent ($7 / $3 = 233%)
Gross profit as a percentage of sales = 70 percent ($7 / $10 = 70%)

Now let's continue to examine the P&L statement for ABC Hat Company with the above assumptions in mind.

Observation 1

- Sales and COGS are above budget in gross dollars for the month—sales by $6,000 and COGS by $1,000.
- Gross profit is above expectations for the month by $5,000. (The actual gross profit of $17,500 minus the expected profit of $12,500 leaves $5,000).
- Actual COGS were 30 percent of sales for the month. (COGS $7,500 / sales of $25,000 = 30%).

- Budgeted COGS for the month was 34 percent of sales. (COGS $6,500 / sales of $19,000 = 34%).

The numbers can tell you the story of your company's performance. As I've said, think of accounting as a way to take the pulse of your business. The numbers above provide a great example of how COGS can be higher than the plan in whole dollars ($1,000), but actually below budget as a percentage of sales for the month (actual equaling 30 percent versus the budgeted 34 percent). Additionally, as illustrated below, the gross profit for the month of May (sometimes called product margin) is above the budget not only in total dollars but also as a percentage of sales:

Actual—gross profit of $17,500 / sales of $25,000 = 70%
Budget—gross profit of $12,500 / sales of $19,000 = 66%

As you may have guessed, it's the ratio between sales and COGS that is most important when analyzing the numbers on a P&L statement, not necessarily the whole dollars. For example, if your sales revenue is above plan for the month (and this is not due to retail price increases and you did not incur an increase in your hat costs), you would then expect your product COGS to be above budget in whole dollars proportionate to the increased revenue because you sold more goods (hats) than was budgeted. In this case, the COGS would increase three dollars above budget for every extra hat that was sold above the plan.

And if we look even further, we can learn that because COGS was up one $1,000 for the month (and we again assume there was no increase in our product costs) the company sold 333 more hats in May than was budgeted (COGS $1,000 / hat costs $3 = 333 hats). If we drill down even further, we can calculate that these extra hats theoretically brought in $3,330 in revenue (333 hats × $10 per hat = $3,330). Naturally, this does not take inventory shrinkage into account.

However, since gross sales were above plan by $6,000 for the month, and the ostensible additional hat sales brought in only a little over half of that amount ($3,330), we can then assume that the company implemented a resale price hike on its hats at some point during the month of May to explain the additional sales revenue.

Observation 2

- Actual YTD COGS are above budget in total dollars by $15,000 and as a percentage of sales by 8 percent (*actual 38 percent of sales versus the budgeted 30 percent).

Actual—COGS $47,500 / sales of $125,000 = 38%

Budget—COGS $32,500 / sales of $110,000 = 30%

There are several factors that may have caused these higher YTD product costs:

- An unexpected increase in product costs early in the fiscal year that was not captured in the budget could explain the increase.
- Higher-than-expected product theft, waste, or defective products not reflected in the budget could account for the disparity between the actual numbers and the budgeted numbers. Inventory shrinkage boosts COGS.
- Higher-than-budgeted sales will cause higher product costs in whole dollars. Price discounting not factored into the budget will cause product costs to be above the plan as a percentage of sales. This concept assumes sales discounting costs were reflected in COGS, and not posted to a promotional discount expense line item on the P&L statement.

Observation 3

- The company is carrying very high levels of inventory each month in terms of total dollar value versus its monthly sales.

As I noted above, we have assumed that ABC's month-end inventory value has averaged $20,000 for the past year. Calculate month-end inventory value by counting all available product stock for resale in a company's possession at the end of the month. Then add up the value of the product. Don't confuse this with the method for calculating COGS (please see appendix C for calculating COGS). The current P&L statement reflects an average monthly COGS of $9,500.

May YTD COGS of $47,500 / 5 months = $9,500

In most cases, month-end inventory value is a fair indicator of the average inventory value a company is carrying throughout the month.

With this information we can conclude that the ABC Hat Company is selling only half of its average month-end inventory value in any given month.

$9,500 average monthly COGS / average month-end inventory of $20,000 = 47.5%

Clearly, the company is carrying an excessive amount of product. Ideally, a company should carry as little inventory as possible without running out of a specific item prior to the next delivery of goods, thus maximizing inventory turnover within a fiscal period.

For example, wouldn't you prefer to take the three dollars it costs ABC Hat Company to purchase a hat and turn it into a ten-dollar sale two or three times in the course of a month (hence, turning your inventory over two or three times in a month) rather than tie your money up in unnecessary excessive levels of product inventory? Since the company orders and receives hats on a weekly basis, it would appear that it would have little problem reducing inventory levels down by as much as 80 percent. That is to say the company should not have to carry much more than $3,200 worth of inventory at any given time. That's the case because it sells only about $2,400 worth of product per week.

In a perfect retail world, ABC Hat Company would know in advance the exact number of hats it would sell each week by size, style, and color. It would place the product order every week one week in advance of receiving the goods. This would result in turning the entire inventory over one time each week (four times per month) with a theoretical inventory value of zero at the end of each week and each month (just moments before receiving their next delivery). Unfortunately, this is not a realistic expectation for ABC Hat Company, or most any other company, for that matter. You always are going to have to carry extra inventory. The trick is to figure out how to carry as little extra inventory as possible.

Historical sales are a good predictor of future sales and the product needs for most companies. For the ABC Hat Company, maintaining an average starting inventory value that is 35 percent higher than its expected sales each week should be a reasonable goal to attain. You might call this "just in time" delivery with a 35 percent inventory cushion. In ABC's situation, that equates to maintaining a starting inventory of about $3,206 each week.

average monthly COGS as calculated above $9,500 / 4 weeks = $2,375
$2,375 × 35% = $831
$831 + $2,375 = $3,206

This reduction in inventory is significant, and it would be a great benefit to the company. The new inventory strategy would result in turning the product inventory over a healthy three times per month.

average monthly COGS / average month-end inventory value
$9,500 / $3,206 = 3

The nearly $17,000 savings in inventory-carrying costs could then be used for other business needs, or it could be invested in good mutual funds for the owner's benefit.

Consider the benefits to a larger company carrying hundreds of thousands of dollars in product inventory if it could successfully manage inventory levels down to just-in-time delivery while allowing for a reasonable inventory cushion. Minimum inventory levels free up valuable cash and warehouse space, and they also reduce labor costs associated with ordering, receiving, rotating, and counting excess inventory. For businesses working with fresh food items, which will spoil in a relatively short period of time or that have "best if used by" dates stamped on the package, excess inventory can be particularly problematic. These companies will suffer the additional loss of having to throw out product as it spoils or ages beyond noted dates (inventory shrinkage).

In spite of the benefits, many business owners and managers don't bother to properly manage their inventory. They buy what they want, when they want it, and they don't seem to consider the bottom line. They don't track what they have on hand, and they end up buying duplicate items that often get stuck on a shelf and lost to the world for years. Some managers believe it's not necessary to invest time and money into managing their cost of goods and product inventory on a continuous basis, which is about the worst thing you can do if inventory falls under part of your management duties. In my opinion, owners and managers cannot afford not to manage their inventory. Failure to do so, as we saw with the ABC Hat Company, can end up creating built-in inefficiencies that get in the way of how a business operates.

As noted, every company should implement an inventory control program appropriate for its specific needs and budget. And don't forget to zero in on the seemingly small picture too. I can't tell you how many managers I've met who took the time to implement a bare-bones inventory control and tracking system, but then failed to track and include what they perceived to be small incidental parts and supplies in their inventory counts. They also didn't charge the customer when those parts were part of a job, all to the detriment of the financial health of their companies. Inventory is like cash. Manage it wisely. Most of these inventory management concepts can be applied to virtually any business or industry. It will always require some effort, discipline, and commitment within the management team to implement and manage effectively over the long term, but in my experience it is worth it.

As you can see, reading and understanding a P&L statement can lead you to make sound decisions for your business unit or department with regard to inventory tracking and control, identifying positive and negative trends, and keeping an eye on costs versus revenue.

Wading into the realm of basic accounting can be a little intimidating at first, but over time, analyzing the numbers will become second nature for you.

Please see appendix C for business math sample formulas.

Tips in a Nutshell

- A profit and loss statement is like a report card on a company's performance for a given time period.
- Terms used on P&L statements can vary, but the concept of tracking revenue and costs remains constant.
- Understand what drives the numbers. They'll tell a story about the company's performance.
- Tracking and controlling inventory can save money and boost profitability.
- Inventory shrinkage (the loss of inventory due to non-sales events) cuts into the bottom line and adds to the cost of goods.
- Historic sales are good indicators of future sales in a given month, and they can help establish appropriate inventory levels for that month.
- Consider the fact that every inventory dollar your company loses in a given day is a dollar off your bottom line. And it is lost forever. Collectively these dollars might be the margin you require to making a reasonable profit. Visualize your company's product line as consisting of brand-new, crisp one- and five-dollar bills wrapped in $100 and $500 bundles. If this were the case, wouldn't you take all the steps necessary to ensure your inventory was secured and accounted for each and every day? Sure, you would. Which is my point, it should not matter if your inventory consists of bundles of cash or baseballs and bats worth one- and five-dollars each respectively. All products, regardless of what they are, have real value and should be treated like cash.

||

Safety First

Management encompasses a wide range of responsibilities, and the higher up the corporate ladder you climb, the more diversified and specialized those responsibilities are likely to be. Let's add one last task to your already full plate—employee safety. It may seem obvious, but it is definitely worth emphatically saying that safety in the workplace is of paramount importance. Of course, a secretary won't face the same risks at work as a roofer perched atop a house with a nail gun, but you never know. Strange things happen all the time. I've seen my share of weird stuff over the years, and almost nothing surprises me anymore. The point is that as a new manager you are going to bear some responsibility for safety in your business unit, and it would be good for you to give that some thought right now as you read this chapter.

If you don't think safety issues can jump up and bite you on the butt, guess again. We once had an office staffer who hurried down a flight of stairs while talking on her cell phone. She held the phone with one hand and carried her lunch and drink in the other. She tripped, was unable to grab the handrail, and fell. Her injuries put her out of work for about ten weeks. That incident cost our company a fair amount of money, including higher workers' compensation insurance rates and the added expense of employing and training temporary help. Soft costs included the extra time required of other personnel to properly investigate the accident and process the claim from the time of the incident to closing the case. We experienced a reduction in operating efficiencies associated with having a minimally trained person working the very important receptionist desk. Unfortunately, the absence of our highly trained employee also negatively affected our ability to consistently deliver superior customer care and services to our existing clients. That caused a significant loss in sales and other business opportunities, all because of one silly mistake.

Promoting safety in the workplace reduces the odds of costly accidents.

Actively promoting safety in the workplace is an area many frontline managers ignore. It is also an area that does not always get promoted or supported from the top down. Ask most managers if safety is a priority where they work, and they'll usually say it is. However, when you inspect their workers' compensation case history, written safety program, and the level of safety enhancement activity in the company, you'll see that in reality many actually do a poor job of promoting safety. While the average number of accidents per employee will vary from one industry to another, safety should always receive high priority across the board.

In addition to higher workers' compensation insurance rates, sick leave, hiring temporary help, and so on, employee-caused accidents can expose your company to possible civil lawsuits should an incident result in bodily injury to someone outside your organization. That will cause an increase in the cost of the company's general liability insurance. Of course, you would also incur the additional costs incurred to repair or replace property damaged during an employee-related incident.

Does your company have a safety program?

If you have taken a position in a large corporation, or at a franchise, chances are safety protocols are in place where you work. The question is whether anyone actually follows them. You don't want to raise a fuss about it during your first week at work, but you can quietly make your direct reports aware of the program, and you can make it clear that you take the program seriously. Just doing that will go a long way toward promoting safety in the workplace since your employees will know you aren't kidding around when you tell them you want the program followed to the letter.

If your company does not have an active safety program, share your safety ideas with your manager. After receiving your manager's blessing, utilize the information in this chapter to customize a safety program that best meets your current business needs.

The most difficult task you'll have in moving forward with a new safety program will be educating, training, and selling the concept of preventable versus non-preventable accidents. Managers and employees alike often struggle with this concept. Managers frequently stick up for members of their teams (not unlike the way some parents think their kids can do no wrong), and they'll tend to brush off the deeper implications of a potential incident or accident. "Oh, nobody's going to slip on that," the manager will say. "We watch where we're going!" Trust me, somebody is going to slip and break a bone. If the floor is wet, you've got an accident waiting to happen.

For the most part, employees think all accidents are just that— accidents that can't be prevented. "Hey, accidents happen! What do you expect me to do about it?" they'll ask. The fact is that virtually all accidents are not accidents at all. They are almost always incidents that would not have occurred with the proper adherence to safety protocols. If you make sure the floor isn't wet, then people will be less likely to slip and fall.

Most accidents are preventable, and from a safety standpoint, those are the ones you want to focus on.

Before I get into the nuts and bolts of how a safety program works, first let's recognize that there are risks in everything we do, including getting out of bed in the morning, tying our shoes, cooking dinner, and driving or walking to work, to name a few. Second, people don't set out to perform tasks with the intention of hurting themselves or others. But unfortunately, they do.

Many of the tasks we carry out are routine, and we successfully complete these responsibilities without much thought or concern for our safety. But given enough time, even the ordinary can get dangerous. Problems can also arise when we take on new tasks but don't know exactly what we're doing. We also can get into trouble when we try unconventional ways to get something done, and it backfires on us.

When someone proceeds to do a job, that person essentially assumes all responsibilities for accurately determining that he or she has the required skills, appropriate equipment, and safety competence to complete the task successfully. When a person miscalculates his or her ability to do a job, becomes careless, or fails to employ appropriate care and caution, and the person's actions result in personal injury or property damage, he or she is at fault for what should be considered a preventable accident.

For example, if you take it upon yourself to utilize specialized power equipment without proper training and you injure yourself or others, you'd be at fault. That would be a preventable accident. If you don't follow safe-lifting procedures and you hurt your back, that's a preventable accident. If you don't look both ways when driving through an intersection, even if you have a green light, and you get T-boned by an oncoming ambulance, that's a preventable accident.

Non-preventable accidents do happen, but they're as rare as a blue moon. If a meteorite falling to earth hits a car causing it to crash, that would be considered a non-preventable accident. When an out-of-control vehicle creams you while you are sitting at a red light, that's non-preventable in that there was nothing you could have done to prevent the accident. If you are in perfect shape and you're following all the proper lifting procedures and you *still* hurt your back, that's a non-preventable accident. So, non-preventable accidents do happen, but as I've said, in the majority of cases, the simple use of common sense and caution would have prevented these incidents from happening.

Remember, we are not trying to determine who is legally at fault in an accident case. The safety program simply requires an accurate determination as to whether the accident was preventable or non-preventable. A safety committee formed for this purpose would decide. If it is deemed that the accident was preventable, then it's possible that a warning would go into the employee's personnel file. The idea is to set up a safety program that informs, trains, and encourages employees to adhere to safe practices in the workplace and makes clear to employees that there will be consequences if they don't.

If you handle it properly, creating and implementing a company safety program can make for a fun and safe work environment for all employees.

Now let's get into the basics of what your safety program should accomplish. As I mentioned above, making the distinction between a preventable and non-preventable accident is going to be important. If an incident/accident could not have been avoided, then there will be no need to hold the employee responsible. But if an incident/accident was preventable, then that's a different story. A safety program is not all about blame, by the way. It's about raising employee awareness of the importance of following safety protocols and about the fact that disciplinary action could result if those safety protocols are not followed. The intent and spirit of your company's safety program is to create, maintain, and promote a clean and safe work environment for all employees with a primary objective of minimizing (or, ideally, eliminating) preventable accidents. It's just that simple.

The heart of your program will consist of a company-wide safety committee made up of one manager and one non-manager from each department, or some variation of that combination subject to the size and culture of your business. Ask a manager or a representative from your human resources department to chair the committee. Set it up so that the committee meets every other month to discuss and remedy company safety concerns brought forward by committee members. They can also review all work-related personnel and vehicle accidents to determine if the incidents could have been avoided if the employees who were involved had been more cautious.

The immediate supervisors of individuals involved in work-related accidents should investigate such incidents using an accident investigation form (see Appendix B for a sample form). These same managers will be required to attend the next scheduled safety meeting, subsequent to the accident their employee was involved in, to present and discuss the facts of that particular incident. Employees involved in such incidents are also encouraged to attend, but they are not required to do so. The committee will then review the facts, ask questions, and actively discuss the incident.

After that, a vote will be taken to determine if the accident could have been prevented if more caution had been utilized. If an accident is deemed preventable, the involved employee must receive counsel from his or her manager. The manager will have to prepare a written counseling notice (see Appendix B for a sample) and review the circumstances involved in the incident along with the reasons why it was deemed preventable. The employee must be advised that multiple accidents, due to neglect or carelessness, will not be tolerated. The team member may also receive follow-up training appropriate for the incident. For instance, someone who injures his or her back in a preventable incident can watch a video that describes proper lifting techniques. The employee should be made aware that accidents that have been deemed preventable could result in disciplinary action. In fact, this information should be made known to everyone as soon as the program is written up and launched.

Taking the initiative to create and implement a safety program for your company will give you exposure to upper management. You will be seen as proactive and confident. Don't go in like a bull in a china cabinet, though. Be sensitive, articulate, and confident as you go about getting the job done.

If a safety program has teeth, team members are more likely to follow it.

People may have every intention of following the safety program, but they may become lazy and as a result fail to adhere to all procedures. They might ignore you altogether, especially if you are a new manager. If you make sure there are consequences for preventable accidents, you'll be more likely to get the results you're looking for. Within a rolling twelve-month period, employees found to be involved in preventable accidents should be counseled as follows:

First incident: A formal warning is issued to the employee.

Second incident: A second formal warning is issued to the employee.

Third incident: A third formal warning is issued to the employee. The employee is made aware that he or she is now subject to disciplinary action up to and including suspension.

Fourth incident: A fourth formal warning is issued to the employee subject to disciplinary action up to and including termination of employment.

You will need to document all warnings in writing, have the employee sign each notice, and then put each document in his or her personnel file.

These are general guidelines. Depending on the circumstances of a particular incident, a more or less severe penalty may be appropriate. If the preventable accident is really minor, then just talking to the employee is enough, at least at first. If a pattern of accidents develops, then it's time to get more serious about documenting the accidents and warning the employee to be more careful. An employee could be suspended or fired for a first incident that involved gross negligence resulting in serious injury or death, or significant property damage.

As noted above, the safety committee also discusses other safety concerns brought forward by committee members. Some safety issues will be addressed and fully resolved at the meeting. Other concerns may require some research or direction from someone not in attendance before corrective action can be taken. In any event, all covered topics should be identified and noted in the meeting minutes, along with all open safety issues requiring follow-up work. I have provided a sample outline of meeting minutes for your review in Appendix B. The minutes should be reviewed at the start of each subsequent safety meeting.

Below are some additional tips for you to consider. Some obviously won't apply to you if you are running a computer software development department, as opposed to a machine shop or some other industrial enterprise. Others will certainly apply directly to you.

- An important policy in your safety program should stipulate that any employee involved in an accident should report it to his or her direct manager immediately or as soon as possible.

- The appropriate manager must fill out the incident/accident report (see Appendix B) within twenty-four hours of the incident/accident. In my world, I prefer the direct manager of those employees involved in an accident to be the one responsible for carrying out the investigation and filling out the incident/accident report. Of course, following very serious incidents, human resources and other senior managers would involve themselves to ensure that all the facts relative to the accident are properly documented.

- Some companies require employees who are involved in any reportable incident/accident to immediately get tested for drugs and alcohol. Others require the test only if bodily injuries are reported. My suggestion is to require a drug/alcohol test for accidents that cause bodily injury or significant property damage or if there are indications that the employee might be under the influence of drugs or alcohol.

- Document all safety meetings and training events. You want to be able to prove an employee has received appropriate training regarding specific safety techniques, policies, and procedures. This will come in handy if you have a future dispute with the employee about safety practices or if you have to provide evidence to agents from the US Department of Labor's Occupational Safety and Health Administration (OSHA).

- If it's required, make sure your employees always wear safety glasses, gloves, footwear, back braces, earplugs, and other such items to protect their health and welfare.

- Always take employee safety concerns seriously. If someone points out a potentially hazardous practice, procedure, or piece of equipment, then address it right away. Don't blow something off only to have it come back and haunt you at a later time. As I always say, I would much rather invest a little more time, effort, and dollars on the front end of an issue while it is still minor than scurry about trying to put a fire out after the fact. Ignoring any problem in business can cost the company big bucks, and that's particularly true when it comes to safety issues.

- Be certain that employees using power equipment have been properly trained and follow all the recommended safety precautions and procedures.

- Insist that managers and employees keep their respective work areas clean, neat, and organized at all times. Nothing should be placed on the floor that could create a trip hazard. Everything should have an appropriate storage place.

There are other safety initiatives you must incorporate into your company's safety program, such as those required by OSHA. Make your team aware of the current requirements, and keep up to date on any changes. For example, depending on your business, one of the more prominent rules of OSHA concerns the Hazard Communication Standard Act. Virtually all employers with hazardous chemicals in their workplace are required to have a hazard communication standard program in place. Become fully familiar with these rules. There are many different components you need to be aware of. Their website is www.OSHA.gov.

Periodically reminding employees about safety issues during staff meetings will reinforce the fact that safety matters to you and the company.

I recommend that, in addition to implementing the safety program, managers include a brief safety discussion at their monthly department meetings (not necessarily every month, but perhaps once a quarter). I also suggest that managers hold a safety presentation meeting once every year with their respective team members and peers. Information presented can include anything that's safety oriented, with meetings lasting thirty to sixty minutes. For example, these presentations might cover subjects such as a review of how to read and utilize material safety data sheets, emergency building evacuation procedures, proper use of fire extinguishers, proper lifting and bending techniques and other topics that might be unique to your business.

To help make your point more clearly, consider procuring safety brochures from various organizations to use in your presentation as handouts. You may want to encourage employee participation, for example, asking employees to demonstrate proper lifting and bending techniques or whatever might be relevant in your department. You might also consider making arrangements for outside speakers to come to your place of business to discuss specific safety matters. Representatives from your local fire and police departments or from your firm's insurance company are good bets. Subject to the size of your business and corporate culture, consider assigning groups of employees the responsibility for developing and facilitating these presentations.

If you are working for a fairly large company or if you are currently experiencing a high rate of preventable incidents; consider creating a spreadsheet (summary report) to track both preventable and non-preventable accidents. Information recorded for each incident should include the name of each involved employee, the department he or she works in, and the nature of the incident, noting if it resulted in personal injury or property damage, or if a vehicle was involved in the incident/accident. I also suggest that you list incidents in chronological order and maintain a rolling twelve-month history of data. This information will be very helpful in identifying company trends (good and bad), and it will serve as a quick reference to use in identifying an employee's personal on-the-job history of incidents/accidents.

Ensuring safety in the workplace isn't rocket science, which is why I am always so surprised about how many managers seem to forget all about it. Don't make that mistake. Those are the kinds of mistakes that can cost your company lots of money, result in civil or criminal charges, and even injury or death to a member of your team or to someone outside the organization. Safety is serious business.

Tips in a Nutshell

- Your entire safety program should be written up and presented to all employees as an expected standard operating procedure.
- Failure to actively encourage safety in the workplace can lead to big financial losses for the company.
- Most incidents/accidents are preventable.
- Make sure your team follows the company's safety program. If none exists or if the existing program lacks substance, discuss your safety program ideas with your manager.
- Staff meetings are a good place to remind your team about the importance of following safety practices in the workplace.
- Consider providing a pizza lunch to all employees after every safety committee meeting in which there are no preventable accidents reported.

12

You're Moving On Up

A successful career in management does not require an MBA or some rare talent. It just requires a basket of essential skills and traits that you probably already possess—being good with people, clearly communicating, paying attention to details, meeting deadlines, keeping a cool head under pressure, and searching out ways to save the company money while solving problems. Now that may sound like a tall order, but it really isn't. If you are weak in one area, the first major step to improving is recognizing the shortcoming and then getting right to work on strengthening that aspect of your management skill set. It doesn't take a genius to do that, but it does take someone with enough self-motivation to move forward. None of us comes into a management job fully formed and perfected. After all, we're just people, like the members of our teams, and we have to learn how to do better and better just like they do. The point is you can do it! You *are* doing it!

For me, managing businesses of all kinds throughout my career has been one of the most rewarding parts of my life. I love the challenge of it all. Running a company is almost like presiding over a giant jigsaw puzzle with the pieces constantly in motion. Just when I think I've fit them all together to create a fine-looking picture, the dazzling image of a well-oiled machine chugging smoothly along, something happens to mix up all the pieces, forcing me to look at everything again from a new perspective. It is the ever-changing nature of business that fascinates me—the people, the marketplace, the products and services. If all of those pieces of the puzzle stayed put for too long, I'd get bored.

Obviously, I'm not saying I welcome problems. Change doesn't always equate to trouble. I'm just saying change keeps things interesting, and I encourage you to welcome it instead of shying away from it. If you're running your company or department properly, change should come about as a matter of course. It should be the result of a systematic process of evaluating yourself, your team, your customers, your market, your competitors, your level of customer service, and the nature of your product or service, and then acting on what you discover to make things better for the good of the company. If you are doing that, then in most cases you will institute changes before problems arise. And if problems do come up, as they always do, you will be adaptive, quick thinking, and ready to address whatever comes.

On the personal side, managing businesses has enabled me to lead a relatively prosperous life. Running companies is about a personal challenge for me, as I've said, but I have never lost sight of the fact that the whole exercise is about making money for the company, myself, and everyone else who works with me—all of that *and* providing what the customer wants. Earning a good salary with benefits and being able to save for retirement are big pluses to a successful career in management. But the acquisition of material wealth isn't necessarily what should be driving you. The best managers know they're going to get paid well, but they do what they do mostly because being a manager is who they are in the first place, right down to their bones. They get a kick out of the hunt, the business, and the people they work with, and they like to solve problems and come up with innovative ways to enhance profitability.

With the right attitude, you can go far as a manager. You've taken your first big step in getting hired as a manager or you are preparing to position yourself to take that step in the near future. The way ahead is not going to be easy. After all, if everyone could be the boss, we'd have too many cooks in the kitchen, and nothing would get done. Not everyone is cut out to be a manager, but I am confident that you are. So, on those days when you feel overwhelmed, rest assured that I have felt that way many times before, and it won't surprise me if I feel that way again. I've gotten through it, and so can you.

As you become more highly skilled in all the management techniques we've discussed in this book, your job will get easier. You'll enjoy it even more than you do now. You'll get noticed. With luck and hard work, soon you'll be moving on up the corporate ladder to a lifelong rewarding career in management. You're already well on your way!

Appendix A: Employee Sample Documents

Your company will probably have standardized disciplinary report forms, employment ad templates, job descriptions, minimum performance standards, and hiring letters, but I've included these documents and other documents in this appendix just in case you need them. At the very least, they'll give you ideas about how to create your own set of employee-related documents.

Sample employment ad with filters

Remember, a filter is something you put in an ad to weed out certain candidates, or to steer certain candidates toward the job. In this example, a landmark near the job site is listed with the hope of discouraging candidates who live too far away.

Warehouse Manager for large vending company
located near the Albany Airport. 2 yr. min. warehouse
management exp. A professional who possesses excellent
people, communication, organization, and problem-solving skills.
Excellent career opportunity. E-mail or fax résumé to
ABC Vending Inc. at —

Sample new-hire welcome letter

Upon receiving the employee's acceptance of a job offer, verbally confirm the start date, and the other terms and conditions of employment you have established with your new employee. Where appropriate (usually for managerial positions) follow up with a welcome letter. The sample below includes a lot about an incentive package linked to the company's safety program. If you have detailed any special offers, incentives, or bonuses during the interview and hiring process, it's a good idea to repeat them in the welcome letter. Otherwise, just welcome the person aboard, and briefly reiterate the job the person was hired to do.

Date
Employee name
Employee address

Dear _____:

I would like to take this opportunity to welcome you to ABC Vending as our new warehouse manager. I am excited to have you on our team and look forward to the positive contributions you'll soon be making to our organization.

As we discussed, I have listed the financial terms of your employment below.

- Start Date: Your first day of employment will be [date].

- Base Pay: [annual pay rate].

- Incentive: [If the position qualifies for one, briefly describe the incentive here].

The incentive is tied to our safety program and will be adjusted as follows: for every incident or accident the safety committee deems preventable for your direct employees beginning [date], your incentive earnings will be reduced by (?) percent, beginning with the third incident.

The incentive, if earned, will be paid after the year-end P&L has been produced. Payment is contingent on your continued employment in good standing throughout the entire year of [year] and at the time incentive is paid.

Once again, I want to welcome you to our organization and wish you much success with your new position.

Sincerely,

Manager's name
Title
Company name

Sample post-interview applicant rejection letter

Although it is often overlooked these days, sending a cordial letter to potential applicants who got far enough for an interview but who weren't hired is a good idea. You should show the same level of professionalism you were expecting from these candidates during the interview process. Thank them for coming in to discuss their qualifications for the opportunity you were offering. Remember, you may want to hire one of these prospects in the future, and that day can sometimes come much sooner than you might think. Be professional and always treat potential talent with sensitivity and respect.

Date
Applicant's name
Applicant's address

Dear:

Thank you for the interest you have shown in considering a position here at ABC Vending Inc. I appreciate your taking the time to meet with me to discuss employment opportunities and your qualifications for the job. Although your experience and qualifications are impressive, we have made the difficult decision to hire another individual whose qualifications best meet our needs at this time.

Your résumé will remain active in our files for one year, and you will be considered for future opportunities at ABC Vending Inc.

Your regard for our organization is greatly appreciated. Please accept our best wishes for your continued career success.

Sincerely,

Manager name
Title
Company name

Sample job description

Even simple jobs should be written up. Include the duties, expectations, safety program adherence policy, and other key company standards.

ABC Vending Inc.
Job Description

Position: Warehouse Manager

Reports to: General Manager

Job Summary: Design, implement, and manage policies and procedures for the warehouse to effect maximum operating efficiencies, and effective product inventory control systems while achieving a high level of internal customer satisfaction.

Qualifications: 1. Two years of warehouse management experience.
2. Excellent people, communication, organization, and problem-solving skills.
3. Working knowledge of common computer applications.
4. Ability to frequently lift up to fifty pounds in the course of one day.
5. Must be able to squat, bend, and walk for long periods of time.
6. High school graduate.

Responsibilities: 1. Ensure all assigned employees have, are familiar with, and adhere to their respective job descriptions.
2. Monitor and evaluate the job performance of all assigned employees (train, coach,

and counsel as necessary). Conduct annual employee reviews.

3. Carry out monthly department meetings.

4. Maintain a thorough understanding of the business category through industry publications, continuing education, and convention attendance.

5. As the company's merchandise buyer, manage inventory shrinkage and product levels to the company plan. Avoid over and out-of-stock conditions while negotiating the lowest product costs possible with suppliers. Pursue all available product rebate programs offered by manufacturers and suppliers.

6. Manage the security of company buildings, vehicles, and other company assets.

7. Manage the repair, maintenance, and upkeep of building and grounds. Maintain areas in a neat, clean, and organized condition.

8. Review, approve, and manage all account payables relative to assigned areas of accountability in accordance with company policy.

9. Ensure the company is in full compliance with all OSHA and Employee Right-to-Know regulations.

10. Assist general manager in administering the company's safety program.

11. Oversee the company's vehicle maintenance and repair program.

12. Take on special projects as assigned by general manager.

Note: Job description is subject to change.

Sample preprinted non-management disciplinary/counseling form

I typically use the following form for non-management personnel who are being disciplined for violating company policies and procedures or who are being counseled for poor work performance or competency concerns and issues. Be sure to note the dates of the rule violations and the dates of any formal disciplinary/counseling meetings you may have had with the employee in the first section of this form (where you discuss your concerns).

Employee Disciplinary/Counseling Notice

Employee's Name: _____

Date of notice: _____

Work performance concerns: _____   Company rule violation: _____

_____
_____
_____
_____
_____
_____

Counseling and/or disciplinary corrective action plan:

_____
_____
_____
_____
_____
_____
_____

Follow-up and next steps:

_____
_____

Douglas J. West

_____
_____
_____
_____
_____

Employee's remarks:

_____
_____
_____
_____
_____
_____
_____

_____   _____
Employee Signature   Manager Signature

cc: Employee personnel file

Sample management disciplinary/counseling memo

The following memo is the standard format I prefer to use when disciplining or counseling a manager for any concerns or issues I may have. In the case below, the employee is about to be terminated. Obviously, you'll have to customize each memo for each case. Remember, it's good to be firm as a manager, but in letters like these just state the facts and the dates.

Date:

To: Struggling employee

From: Counseling manager

Re: Job performance review meeting on [date]

As we discussed yesterday, I continue to have many concerns with your work performance, which I have outlined below:

- Your communication and follow-up skills with your peers and customers continue to be unacceptable, both in content (lack of detail) and in the tardiness of returned phone calls and e-mails.

- You continue to procrastinate on completing assigned and routine tasks. For example, employee performance reviews are always late, and you fail to hold effective department meetings with your employees on a regular basis.

- Your department continues to perform inadequately in terms of quality of work and meeting contractual obligations in a timely manner. You need to provide more management oversight.

All these concerns have been discussed with you several times over the past two months, including two formal meetings beginning on [date] of this year. I have provided you with follow-up written details of these meetings outlining the areas of concern and the minimum standards and expectations I have for the position you hold. Unfortunately, you have mostly chosen to disregard my direction and efforts to help you succeed, and regrettably your job performance continues to be unacceptable.

Consequently, your failure to achieve significant improvement in all of the areas noted above within the next thirty days will result in your termination of employment with our company.

_____
Employee signature

Sample minimum performance standards document

Establishing minimum performance standards lets your team members know what you expect of them. Writing out the minimum requirements of a job also provides proof that the employees knew about those minimum standards. In other words, nobody can say they didn't know they were supposed to be doing one thing or another. Every employee should receive and sign a minimum performance standards document when they are hired or promoted to a new position within the company. A copy of the document should be included in the employee's personnel file.

ABC Sales Company

Minimum Performance Standards for Sales and Customer Service Personnel

1. Project a professional and positive image of yourself, the company, and team members at all times. Be polite and courteous even during difficult situations.

2. Your commitment to external customers should include the following:

    A. Always acknowledge and greet customers enthusiastically and in a friendly manner. Be patient, helpful, and cooperative. Provide adequate empathy when working with customers. Remember to smile, even through the phone.

    B. Take ownership of customer concerns or issues when they are brought to your attention. Follow up appropriately to ensure that the customer's needs have been taken care of.

    C. Determine what is important to our external customers. Use this information to satisfy the needs of existing clients and to identify solutions for addressing and overcoming a prospective customers' resistance to buying our products.

D. Determine customer expectations: How often does our customer prefer to hear from us and by what method: phone, e-mail, US mail, or perhaps a personal visit? What kind of promotional, product, or pricing information is our customer interested in receiving?

E. Respond to all inquires within eighteen hours. Same day is preferred.

F. Always arrive at meetings and appointments prepared and on time. Arriving early is always better.

G. Be knowledgeable about our product line, available inventory, internal processes and procedures, and all associated paperwork.

H. Keep your vehicle and work areas clean, neat, and organized at all times. Spotless is preferred.

I. Exceed customer expectations. Under promise and over service. Stay focused and project enthusiasm when interacting with customers.

3. Explain the sales and purchase process.

A. Explain the entire sales process to our customers. Make it clear that while most sales transactions move forward problem free, sometimes delays or problems can occur.

B. Explain that our job as the customer's sales agent is to help minimize these occurrences and keep all parties informed as we move through the sales and closing process.

    C. Over communicate. Leave nothing to the imagination.

4. Inform your manager of any customer-service issues you identify. Offer ideas and solutions to address the concerns.

5. Keep your manager informed of competitive activity in the marketplace. Offer ideas and solutions for any concerns you identify.

6. Complete assigned projects, tasks, and paperwork accurately and in a timely manner.

7. Comply with all company policies and procedures.

—————————————————————   ————————————————————

Signature   Date

Sample staff meeting minutes

Regular staff meetings are a vital way to establish and maintain excellent communication between you and your team, and among your team members. Impress upon your team that the meetings matter, that attending them on time is part of the job, and that you encourage members to share their business improvement ideas and their concerns with the group. Keeping minutes formalizes the process and also creates a record you can refer back to when checking the status of action items. In the event you have a concern about an employee's progress with a given project, the minutes will serve as a record of what was promised. Appoint a responsible member of your team as secretary for staff meetings, and have that person keep accurate minutes.

Douglas J. West

ABC Sales Inc.

Meeting Minutes

To: Names of meeting attendees

From: Your name
Date: April 11, 2012
Subject: Minutes of our April 10, 2012, manager's meeting

1. As discussed, managers to forward updated job descriptions to Doug by 5.10.12.

2. Typically, Bill W. will be available for service calls until 5:30 p.m. Monday through Friday.

3. Justin to implement weekly cleaning routines for all community ponds by 5.10.12.

4. Sherry will discuss "patrol" cell phone usage with our new security company to determine if current usage is reasonable for the services now being provided. Do they have a written cell phone policy for their employees? Target date: 5.30.12.

5. Justin to remove internal wood structure from Building No. 2, Suite 128. Target date: 5.6.12.

6. As discussed, Kim will write up a pre/post home closing procedure that will include a walk-through of homes prior to closing. After the closing, sales agents will escort buyers to the clubhouse for introductions to our staff, where they will receive welcome information, gate cards, etc. Target date: 5.28.12.

7. By May 28th, Kim will write up and implement a sales recognition program to include:

   A. E-mail blast to all employees announcing a new home sales contract recognizing and congratulating the responsible sales agent.

   B. Buyer introduction to community via announcement in our community newsletter.

   C. The creation of a new Salesperson of the Quarter Award to be presented at our employee quarterly meetings.

Other items discussed:

- View things through the eyes of our customers.
- Pay attention to details.
- Some standards and expectations are nonnegotiable.
- Best practices: Share ideas and best practices with each other.
- Things are not always as they appear.

Our next meeting is scheduled for 9:00 a.m. on Wednesday, May 16, 2012, in the corporate conference room.

cc: [anyone not in attendance who should know about what was discussed]

Appendix B: Safety Program Sample Documents

Effective safety programs require the support of the entire management team. Each manager must make it known to employees that he or she is dedicated to upholding the standards of the safety program, and that it is part of each employee's job to do the same. Each employee should be taught the difference between preventable incidents/ accidents and non-preventable incidents/accidents. Each employee should be informed that disciplinary action is possible if too many preventable accidents occur.

Proper documentation is vital to the effective and efficient operation of a company safety program. Below are documents you will need as you go forward.

Sample accident/incident investigation report

When an incident or accident occurs, the manager of the employee involved should be the one to interview the employee and then fill out a report (see below). This should be done within twenty-four hours of the incident/accident.

ABC Sales Inc.
Incident/Accident Report

Today's date: _____ Date of accident: _____

Employees involved in accident: _____
_____
_____

Employee's description of accident: _____
_____
_____
_____
_____
_____

Date accident was reported to manager: _____

Were there any witnesses to accident? If yes, please list names and telephone numbers.
_____
_____
_____
_____

Location of accident: _____
_____
_____
_____
_____

Did accident result in bodily injury? If yes, please describe: _____
_____
_____
_____
_____

Did accident result in property damage? If yes, please describe:

_____

_____

_____

_____

If the accident involved a vehicle, please include copy of the police report and the following information:

	Company vehicle information	**Other vehicle information**
Driver's name:	_____	_____
Driver's license no.:	_____	_____
Vehicle make/model:	_____	_____
Vehicle VIN No.:	_____	_____

Please describe vehicle accident: _____

_____

_____

_____

Manager's evaluation:

Was employee wearing/using required safety equipment? Yes _____
No _____ N/A _____

What equipment could have been utilized to prevent this accident?

_____

_____

What actions/measures are needed to prevent the recurrence of a similar incident? _____

_____
_____
_____

Employee signature: _____
Date: _____

Manager signature: _____
Date: _____

Sample personnel safety documentation

When an incident/accident occurs, you fill out a report that describes what happened. You also need to document what is said between you and the employee, and that documentation should be placed in the employee's personnel file.

ABC Sales Inc.
Personnel Safety Documentation
(Counseling Notice)

Name: _____

Date: _____

Description of incident: _____
_____
_____

The safety committee recently reviewed the accident you were involved in on [date]_____ and deemed it to be preventable.

This is your _____ preventable incident in the past twelve months.

As you are aware, safety in the workplace is everyone's responsibility. You must use caution and follow company safety procedures at all times. Failure to do so could result in disciplinary action up to and including suspension or discharge as outlined below:

Preventable incidents within a rolling twelve-month period.

First incident   Formal warning to employee.
Second incident   Formal warning to employee.

Third incident	Formal warning to employee subject to disciplinary action up to and including suspension.
Fourth incident	Formal warning to employee subject to disciplinary action up to and including termination of employment.

These are general guidelines. Depending on the nature and circumstances of a particular incident, a more or less severe penalty may be appropriate. For example, an employee could be suspended or discharged for a first incident involving gross negligence that results in serious injury or death or in significant property damage.

Follow-up training: _____
_____
_____
_____
_____

Follow-up training to be completed by:

_____
Date

Received by_____   _____
             Employee Signature   Manager

Sample safety committee meeting minutes

Just as it's important to keep minutes for regular staff meetings, it's important to keep minutes whenever the safety committee meets to discuss safety issues. The minutes provide a record that could be important if a legal dispute with an employee and/or customer occurs.

ABC Sales Inc.
Safety Committee Meeting Minutes

To: [As a way of knowing who was at a particular meeting, I always list those actually in attendance here. This will be very helpful if someone who was there later says he or she was unaware of a given procedure or policy that was discussed during the meeting.]

From: [The person who chaired the meeting]

Date: April 12, 2012

Subject: Minutes of our April 11, 2012, Safety Meeting

----

1. Personal injury incidents reviewed:

Accident Date	Associate	Accident	Ruling
2.24.12	Dennis D.	Twisted ankle getting out of vehicle	Preventable
3.22.12	Don L.	Injured back lifting box	Preventable

2.   Vehicle accidents reviewed:

Accident Date	Associate	Accident	Ruling
2.23.12	Bob B.	Hit road sign, broke mirror on truck	Preventable
3.12.12	Jason W.	Appropriately parked vehicle; hit by another	Non-preventable

3.   Corey W. will test vehicle cargo nets as an alternative to bungee cords prior to our next safety meeting.

4.   Steve W. will acquire decals noting vehicle height and apply them to dashboards of all vehicles by 5.10.12.

5.   Reminder to all employees:

- Drivers must note vehicle equipment defects on their pre- and post-trip reports. Serious defects must be brought to a manager's attention, and necessary repairs must be made prior to continued use of the vehicle.

- Appropriate footwear must be worn at all times while on duty (rubber-bottom, slip-resistant shoes).

- The intent and spirit of our new company safety program and the efforts of our safety committee are to provide a clean and safe work environment for all employees, where our primary objective is to eliminate preventable accidents. Accordingly, I am asking for your continued cooperation and extra efforts in our pursuit to achieve a record of no preventable accidents for a twelve-month time period. This would be a great accomplishment we could all be proud of. To help celebrate our anticipated successes and recognize your efforts, the company will provide a pizza luncheon following every safety meeting in which no preventable accidents are reported.

The next safety meeting is scheduled for June 12, 2012, at 3:00 p.m. in the conference room.

cc: [I copy people who were not at the meeting, but who do have an interest in the information shared and in topics discussed. I always post a copy of the minutes on the employee bulletin board.]

Appendix C: Business Math Sample Formulas

Calculate product COGS as a percent of sales

$100 (product cost) / $400 (retail price) = 0.25 (25% COGS)

Calculate retail price with the known product cost value in dollars and as a percentage of the retail price

$100 (product costs) / 0.25 (25 % COGS) = $400 (retail price)

Calculate retail price with a 25 percent markup

$100 (product cost) × 0.25 (25% markup) =
$25 + $100 = $125 (retail price/markup)

Determine product cost prior to a 25 percent markup

$125 (retail price) / 1.25 = $100 (product cost)

Identify percent of product markup

$125 (retail price) — $100 (COGS) =
$25 / $100 = 0.25 (25% markup)

Determine retail price with a 5 percent tax added in

$100 (retail price) × 0.05 (5% tax) = $5 + $100 = $105

Identify retail price prior to a 5 percent tax being added in

$105 (retail price with tax) / 1.05 = $100 (retail price)

Calculate increase in sales as a percent
of original sales value**

$11,000 (new sales value) — $10,000 (original
sales value) = $1,000 (increase)

$1,000 (increase) / $10,000 (original sales value) = 0.10 (10%)

Calculate a decrease in sales as a
percent of original sales value**

$10,000 (original sales value) — $9,000 (new
sales value) = $1,000 (decrease)

$1,000 (decrease) / $10,000 (original sales value) = 0.10 (10%)

**   The above two formulas can also be used for calculating an increase or decrease in expenses as a percent of the original expense value.

How to Calculate Product Cost of Goods (COGS)

Retailers, such as shoe stores, will usually purchase their "ready to sell" shoes and other allied products throughout the fiscal period (usually consisting of one month) as needed. They'll calculate their COGS at the end of each month using a formula that will identify how many shoes and related products were sold, lost due to theft, and damaged during the financial period. Because shoe stores (like most retailers) maintain a working inventory to draw on, they cannot simply add up the value of the shoes and other merchandise purchased throughout the month and label it their cost of goods. They need to identify their total product COGS and inventory shrinkage; that is the net value of their total available inventory throughout the financial period less the actual inventory value available at the end of the fiscal period:

		Obtained:
Beginning inventory on the 1st of the month	$10,000	(by physical product count)
Plus product purchases throughout the month	+ 5,000	(from product invoices)
Total available inventory for month	15,000	
Less ending inventory on the last day of month	- 7,000	(by physical product count)
Equals cost of goods for the month	$8,000	
(Includes Inventory Shrinkage)		

Taking inventory means taking a physical count of all company-owned product (stock for resale)—on the sales floor, backroom shelves, or wherever it may be. Ideally, inventory should be counted at the end of the last business day of the fiscal period (when all inventory movement and business transactions have stopped). Beginning inventory value is actually the same as the ending inventory value taken at the close of business on the last day of the previous fiscal month. Thus, in this example, the ending inventory of $7,000 will be the beginning inventory for next month's product costs calculations.

Utilizing the above method for calculating COGS will reflect the cost of products sold and product that has spoiled, or been stolen, damaged, or tossed out (inventory shrinkage).